Back to Good

Six Billion Ways to Bring Goodness into Our World, One Person at a Time

Ken Ferrara

Bloomington, IN Milton Keynes, UK

authorHOUSE®

AuthorHouse™
1663 Liberty Drive, Suite 200
Bloomington, IN 47403
www.authorhouse.com
Phone: 1-800-839-8640

AuthorHouse™ UK Ltd.
500 Avebury Boulevard
Central Milton Keynes, MK9 2BE
www.authorhouse.co.uk
Phone: 08001974150

First published by AuthorHouse 1/31/2007

ISBN: 1-4184-7046-5 (e)
ISBN: 1-4184-5346-3 (dj)
ISBN: 1-4184-5345-5 (sc)

Printed in the United States of America
Bloomington, Indiana

This book is printed on acid-free paper.

**Book One in the
Back to Good Series**

~ A Tale of Two Wolves ~

One evening an old Cherokee told his grandson about a battle that goes on inside people.

He said, "My son, the battle is between two wolves inside us all.

The first wolf is evil. It is anger, envy, jealousy, sorrow, regret, greed, arrogance, self-pity, guilt, resentment, inferiority, lies, false pride, superiority, and ego.

The second wolf is good. It is joy, peace, love, hope, serenity, humility, kindness, benevolence, empathy, generosity, truth, compassion, and faith."

The grandson thought about it for a moment and then asked his grandfather, "Which wolf wins?"

The old Cherokee simply replied, "The one you feed."

—Author unknown.

Getting Back to Good will feed your second wolf, while starving the first.

Six Billion Ways to Bring Goodness Into Our World, One Person at a Time.

More than six billion people awaken every day on Earth, and each new dawn brings a gift of renewed opportunity for us to foster goodness toward nature and our fellow human beings. While goodness is encouraged and upheld every day by countless people around the world within every culture, creed, and society, billions of people corrode it with varying degrees of negative, selfish, and evil thoughts and actions. No one can exclusively pass the blame onto others for the selfishness and negativity that exists, because every person takes part in some way, at some time, in contributing to a less than desirable world, and is therefore responsible for improving it.

Imagine the possibilities...

We, all of us, are responsible for living with goodness. Whatever community or country we are a part of, regardless of our personal lifestyles, beliefs, or opinions, each of us can do our part to collectively strengthen the human spirit of goodness. Simple thoughts and actions can bring our world back to good more than six billion times a day, and the potential is exponential when each of us takes part in the effort. Peace, compromise, prosperity, fulfillment, and happiness are the potential harvest when we find and travel unique paths to the common goal of true goodness. Let's work to...

get Back to Good!

Contents

Preface

Who are you? Who do you want to be? What are you meant to do with your life? Are you truly happy and fulfilled or do you feel that life is unfair and difficult? Have you honestly considered these questions? On a larger scale, what is going on in the world? From the vast amounts of negativity and selfishness that are so readily observable, to failing relationships, human suffering, financial troubles, and frightening global issues, it seems that humanity is declining at an ever-increasing rate.

If this is the case, what can one person — what can you do to help reverse this trend? Do you think you can make a difference or do you deem that a naïve belief? What if there was a way for you to effectively create positive changes in our world? What if simple thoughts, actions, and attitudes could empower you with the ability to bring about immensely powerful, beneficial changes to your life, and therefore into our world?

Committing to get back to good can help you achieve these positive goals. In order to set this inspirational process into motion, contemplate the following questions: Why should goodness be part of your life? How does living with goodness benefit you? Is it even possible to become a better person in today's hectic, sometimes unforgiving world? What if you could take a step back from your opinions, circumstances, and daily routines, and learn to be more tolerant, kind, and grateful? What if, above all, you could live with more goodness?

Certainly, you don't have to be good. No laws of humanity dictate that you must be patient, giving, or kind. If you are selfish and intolerant, or show care and concern only for what is important to you, the "goodness police" aren't going to charge you with a crime and take you to jail. After all, life can be so hard, demanding, and seemingly unfair that taking care of your needs may leave little time, ambition, or energy for being a kind, selfless, and giving person. So the question remains: Why should you live with goodness?

Despite the cliché, living with goodness truly becomes its own reward, on a personal level as well as on a grand scale. Actively seeking to become a better person for yourself and for the others around you will move you toward a positive and enriching life in all of its aspects. Choosing to get back to good empowers you to:

- Find happiness and fulfillment;
- Express patience; you'll be able to deal with stressful situations and your relationships more positively;
- Remember what you should be thankful for, from your health to your family and friends to the day itself;
- Show tolerance of the dynamic diversity in our world, from the multitude of differing religious and spiritual beliefs to widely varying personal views and appearances;
- Care for yourself physically, emotionally, and spiritually;
- Mend broken or faltering relationships with family members, as well as with friends and acquaintances;
- Show kindness through the numerous differing circumstances that life inevitably brings, from offering apologies and forgiveness to holding the door open for the person behind you;

> ➢ Find meaning and purpose for life by learning to live for more than yourself;
> ➢ Realize peace of mind by understanding that life is ultimately not in your hands.

Different situations and experiences can certainly make it challenging to live with goodness. However, if you continually focus on maintaining a positive outlook filled with actions of gratitude, that challenge can be met and mastered. This concept is similar to that of trying to live a healthy lifestyle. Everyone knows what *should* be done in order to stay healthy, but the motivation, knowledge, or will to do so may not be very strong. To remain focused on the goal, you would need to read and talk about staying healthy and surround yourself with supportive, positive people. The same holds true for living with goodness: reading about it, discussing it, and doing what is necessary to make it a priority in your life will help you accomplish it.

Ultimately, the ideals of goodness are what people will strive to attain. While no one can achieve those ideals perfectly, the fact that you are trying will earn rewards for you, as well as for the lives you touch. Your life's purpose will become much clearer when you focus time and effort on your responsibility for living with goodness.

~ The Journey Back to Good ~

Getting back to good is an ongoing, lifelong process that can help you personally address and attack negative thoughts and actions, while adding countless positive benefits to your life. You will learn to infuse more selflessness, patience, and compassion into your beliefs and values, which will allow you to become more tolerant, giving, and understanding.

Back to Good shows you why striving toward individual goodness is necessary and provides you with a guided, practical process for achieving it. A multitude of "To Do" checklists create inspiring visual aids and provide tangible directives on how to effectively apply these concepts in everyday life. Fortunately, this process can be customized to fit your life by the person who knows that life best — you! Getting back to good can be used modestly as a tool to improve personal relationships, attitudes, and perspectives, or as a grand device toward helping achieve more harmony in the world.

If you identify at least one area of life where you are able to foster goodness in some way, then this book is well worth the read. Take a close, objective look at yourself to see where you can improve. Regardless of what has happened in the past, you can take actions that move you toward a better life. With the many different hats you wear, whether as a parent, a caring person, a student, a family member, or a friend; whether as a teacher, a religious/spiritual leader or follower, an employee, the head of a company, or the head of a nation, do your part to help bring more goodness into our world. The opportunity is always within reach.

Do not let an encounter with death or tragedy become your wake-up call. Change your thoughts, actions, and life now — don't wait until it is too late. Make amends for any wrongs you have caused and treat others with goodness not because you are forced to, but because it's the right thing to do. Find your way back to good.

All people have a basic decency and goodness. If they listen to it and act on it, they are giving a great deal of what it is the world needs most. It is not complicated, but it takes courage. It takes courage for people to listen to their own good.

—Pablo Casals

From The Author

"Mostly I'm tired of people being ugly to each other."
—John Coffey, from the motion picture, *The Green Mile.*

I like to quote the statement above when people ask me what inspired me to write this book. I was tired of people being mean, impatient, and intolerant, often asking myself, "Why can't people show more kindness and be more giving, trusting, grateful, and understanding? Why can't people just be nice?" Of course, I refused to see that I was responsible for much of the negativity I felt from the nasty looks and comments that I received when driving, or the rude behaviors I witnessed at work and in my own family. I was trapped in a downward spiral of negativity that caused me to be angry, resentful, and selfish.

My motto was, "What's in it for me?!" I was so wrapped up in an "all about me" attitude that I could not see the way I perceived and treated others lacked goodness — that I was treating others in the very ways I found so disheartening. The words I, me, my, and mine were used much too often in my everyday encounters, and self-centered, intolerant behavior served to drain the positive energy and joy from my life. Personal relationships suffered because my actions caused damaging rifts in my family, social, and professional lives.

Following years of stubborn selfishness, and the pain, self-pity, and unhappiness it produced, I began to ask questions. "Why am I so mean and negative at times? Why do I consider my needs to be more important than the needs of others? What can I do to bring more compassion, consideration, and happiness into my life? How can I become a better person, both for myself, as well as for the people around me?" Since *I* was responsible for an abundance of negativity in my life due to my selfish choices and perspectives, only *I* could find the answers to these questions.

Thankfully, after years of self-absorbed confusion, I came to understand that you really do "get what you give," and in order for people to stop being ugly to each other, I must first learn to stop being ugly to others in my life. I finally realized that living with goodness brings positive, productive results and ultimately becomes its own reward. Over the span of a decade, I had reached a very low and scary point in my life, but I overcame that negativity by using the ideas and processes in this book. They helped me improve my perspective and enrich my life, and they can do the same for you.

Back to Good is the combined result of my life experience coupled with the wisdom imparted by those people who consistently embody the best attributes of the human spirit. I have assembled knowledge and lessons I learned from personal struggles, hardships, and times of joy, as well as from examples of countless people who have shown the true goodness we are capable of, into something tangible — something that can help to resolve questions, uncertainties, and challenges of life.

Getting back to good has rewarded me beyond my greatest expectations and has made every day a better day. Of course, life isn't a fairy tale, as hardships and challenges still exist, but faith and guidance have helped me find the goodness and happiness that is available for everyone to enjoy and foster. I embrace the opportunity to inspire people by presenting ways to become more kind, caring, compassionate, and grateful. To that end, this book is my sincere wish to help others find and enjoy the benefits that goodness brings.

~ About the Book ~

You won't find complicated comparisons of differing cultures or religions on these pages, as this book was written to be accessible and beneficial to people of all faiths, and to those who may not have any type of spiritual or religious convictions. I have no intention of imposing my beliefs upon anyone else, because a true spiritual connection is made through one's beliefs and actions of goodness, not through arguments, forceful principles, or disrespect for the various beliefs that exist.

I completely respect the multitude of differing beliefs in our diverse world because everyone travels a personal journey in life and has unique experiences and perspectives.My most heartfelt wish is to respect your views, while offering you the positive, powerful, and practical values that getting back to good can provide. To that end, I made every attempt to express ideas and messages in ways that do not detract from particular beliefs, while at the same time offering a straightforward guide to live with the goodness and tolerance that is native and applicable to every human being. Remember, the principles of getting back to good are fundamentally universal, pertaining to every person, persuasion, and faith.

I am the first to admit that you won't find any astonishing revelations between these covers. Many of the ideas are as old as time, and I am not presenting any new, fundamental beliefs or ideas that have not been written about, thought of, or discussed before. This text contains no earth-shattering insights or complex philosophies. As for myself, I am not a scientist, philosopher, or theologian by trade, and the many advanced ideas and theories of these various fields are admittedly beyond my grasp. That being said, I realize some positions may differ with academia or the scientific community, while others may directly intersect with differing views of spirituality. However, keep in mind that the concepts on these pages ultimately relate to our common link to goodness.

When we focus on getting back to good in personal relationships or in a broader sense, it travels through us into our world. We must seek elemental, idealistic, and collective views that engage other people with compromise, while not segregating or alienating the many different ways others choose to express their views. At the very least, we need to be tolerant of differing perspectives and characteristics, while at the same time learning how to include rather than exclude. We must be tolerant of the fact that different people and different ideas make this world go around. As such, I have attempted to address the responsibility to live with principles that encompass and apply to all people, no matter their race, creed, or country.

Read with an open, optimistic mind, and keep the context of this book in the biggest picture possible. If you feel that living with goodness does not apply to you, you may think quite differently when you draw your last breath. If you believe that getting back to good is too idealistic to foster any meaningful change in our world, then I challenge you to take the energy of that negative perception, put it into thoughts and actions of goodness instead, and see what happens next.

From calling someone you have lost touch with to smiling at the person next to you, *every* good thought and action will help bring our world back to good. Life is too short to wait for the next person to do it; take it upon yourself to be that next person—and pass it on.

Definition

back to good (bak - too - guud), *v.n.* **1.** the choice one makes to be good: *I will commit to live with more goodness.* **2.** the process by which a person connects with SomeThing Greater in order to foster goodness. **3.** to be tolerant of differing spiritual views and beliefs. **4.** to achieve and maintain a perspective of thankfulness for everything in life. **5.** the process by which a person recognizes selfishness and turns it into selflessness. **6.** to give: *help, kindness, tolerance, forgiveness, care for nature, patience, compassion, thankfulness, etc.* **7.** to care for all aspects of health in order to foster goodness. **8.** the process of combining definitions 1–7 to find and fulfill complete purpose for life. **9.** *to get Back to Good.*

CHAPTER 1

Back to Good
We must find our way.

"The welfare of each is bound up in the welfare of all."
—Helen Keller

As we gaze at the dawn of a new millennium, it is easy to see that humanity has gained vast amounts of knowledge and advanced technology. We have more collective power at our disposal than ever before. Ideally, the world should be a nicer place. From the standpoint of our human abilities and achievements, the world should be an abundant, safe, and caring place to live because we have the technical means and ability to care for one another as at no other time in the past. We have the power to eradicate disease, feed the hungry, and make poverty history. While technological advancements and changes are good, we still wrestle with the negative aspects of our own humanity.

Over the course of history, we have epitomized the very definition of goodness by loving, caring, giving selflessly, and showing compassion and tolerance toward one another. The unfortunate reality is that, in many ways, the opposite is also true. We have acted with varying degrees of immorality and evil by choosing to act with selfishness, intolerance, and negativity.

Are selfishness, intolerance, and the darker aspects of human nature simply problems of the human psyche or condition? Where do undesirable thoughts and behaviors come from? What can be done to lessen their growth and eventually slow or even stop their impact? These questions are not easily answered, but we can find answers and put them into practice by accepting that living with goodness is a responsibility that we are accountable for carrying out. Whether or not this responsibility is accepted is another story.

While countless beliefs, philosophies, and rules attempt to govern what is "good," many of us are still lost in the search to find it. We often treat each other with less kindness, patience, and tolerance than we could. When we selfishly concern ourselves with individual needs and desires, we become trapped in a circle of negativity. Viewing life from an overly self-interested perspective causes our needs to become more important than the needs of others, and we allow prejudice, selfishness, and intolerance to flourish.

However...

Day in and day out, people in every society, culture, and spiritual practice are giving, selfless, and kind. For every awful or evil action we become aware of, countless good actions occur. Unfortunately, they often receive little, if any, attention—certainly not the same degree of attention as their negative counterparts of selfishness, violence, and hatred. With the extensive publicity showered on the negative events of our world, one might conclude that human beings are inherently bad, but nothing is further from the truth because the vast majority of humanity is fundamentally good. Nevertheless, there is plenty of room for everyone to act with more goodness and find opportunities to do so in every aspect of life.

Every person can find areas in life where goodness can develop or re-develop. We may be able to repair soured relationships, give to others, or find the motivation to help in one of a million different ways by becoming spiritually, personally, and ideologically tolerant. We must learn to overcome selfishness, eliminate the varying degrees of pain that we cause as well as perceive, and focus on becoming selfless and tolerant. By choosing to embrace good thoughts and actions, more peace, respect, and care is created in our world.

~ **What is Getting Back to Good?** ~

Getting back to good is an ongoing, lifelong process that helps you identify, apply, and attain positive attitudes and actions through *your* particular beliefs and values, while being tolerant of the ways that others do so. This process is not a complete, immediate solution for the troubles and problems of an individual life or for the problems of our world. Rather, it is a set of ideas that can be customized to strengthen personal beliefs and perspectives so they can overcome the negativity that leads away from tolerance, gratitude, and kindness.

Every human being thinks and acts in ways that lead away from goodness to some degree—every human being. As such, the process of getting back to good is not reserved for those who have committed crimes, lived extremely selfishly, or committed illegal or immoral actions. Spiritual, good-natured, and caring people can treat others with less kindness, generosity, respect, and tolerance than is possible. Even essentially good people can produce negativity by caring only for their own.

Fortunately, the vast majority of people exhibit negative or "bad" thoughts and actions that are minor in scope, and require relatively subtle changes in attitude and action to get back to good. Then again, some people wander far from the path of righteousness, committing actions of extreme

3

selfishness, violence, and evil. No matter how an individual has lived or behaved in the past, a path back to good can be found.

****

Making immediate, drastic changes to your life or our world is not necessarily what this process is all about... although it can be.

****

Will getting back to good enable you to fix problems in your life? Yes, troubles, problems, and day-to-day inconveniences can be thoroughly resolved if you make an honest effort to apply the principles of getting back to good. Many challenges you confront may be caused by your thoughts and actions, the way you deal with adversity, and other dilemmas caused by a selfish perspective. However, there will be instances in life where getting back to good cannot resolve the issues you may be facing. In those instances, tend to your troubles by doing what is necessary to fix them, but do so with the care, compassion, and positive attitude that getting back to good emphasizes.

As you find your way, you will realize what is in your life to give to others, and you will remember to be kind, compassionate, and caring, while feeling genuinely thankful. Your perspective can change from one of "What about me?" or "My way is the only way," to one of overwhelming care and concern for others.

~ Back to Goodness ~

The concept of goodness is beyond the scientific and intellectual reach of humankind, and is something that is all encompassing, not overbearing or narrowly focused. It is designed to foster environments where people readily offer kindness, nurture tolerance, and exhibit selflessness. Various cultures have diverse ideas and beliefs that inevitably lead to differing perspectives. While these different outlooks and views have inspired the closeness, co-operation, compassion, and care of the human spirit, they have also spawned separation, prejudice, hatred, and many appalling, heinous actions (ironically, often committed in the name of righteousness).

For centuries, philosophers, theologians, and scholars have debated issues surrounding the true nature of goodness. These discussions give rise to questions such as: "Is goodness fair? Why do bad things happen to good people? Is there more than one type of true spiritual belief?" Some issues these questions call to mind are beyond irrefutable resolution, and best left to experts and opinionarians to debate and attempt to answer. We, however, have more important work to do.

Back to Good does not center on unanswerable questions, complex philosophies, or spiritual separation and exclusion. Rather, it focuses on the responsibility for goodness that every human being shares, and can help answer the following: "Why should I act with goodness, and how can I bring more of it into my life? Why should I accept the fact that others deserve to be treated with respect and tolerance?" The answers to these questions can be difficult to find objectively, yet with patience, practice, and a sincere desire to complete the search, the answers can be found.

~ Our Common Ties ~

We share immense commonality as human beings. Before any race, physical difference, or creed, and before any nationality or mindset, each and every one of us is human—fundamentally common and equal. Who we are, what groups we belong to, or what we do for a living makes no difference, as we all travel over the same ocean called life.

Of course, each of us is on a different type of ship, sailing a different course, but we ultimately travel to the same end.

Every human being comes from the same place, and is heading to the same final destination. For all intents and purposes, we desire the same things from life: to fulfill our needs, to have the ability to love and care for ourselves and our loved ones, to have health, and to believe and connect in our own spiritual way.

Our commonalities dictate that we share life together. As such, the responsibility for living with goodness applies to all human beings equally, from the poor to the rich; from heads of state to followers and leaders of differing spiritual beliefs; from business and community leaders to famous, "powerful," and everyday people. Creed, culture, country, social class, and any other separation or segmentation of the human mind makes no difference; variations in ideology, upbringing, or personality make no difference—everyone is subject to universal laws of goodness. Regardless of status or pursuits in life, those laws equally bind us, and no one is exempt because we are each accountable for our own actions.

****

In the big picture, there is no "us against them," or "you against me." Obviously, you must provide and care for yourself, protect what is yours, and feel connected to people, beliefs, and systems; that's human nature. In the end however, the most crucial battle you will fight is to think and act with goodness — you are accountable for that.

****

Remember, getting back to good is open to many diverse interpretations and possesses a broad, inclusive definition for humanity. A definition that is not exclusively associated with a single spiritual, cultural, or personal view; rather, it applies to everything and everyone, as the universal truths that comprise goodness commonly bind humanity together.

~ Good For Me...Me...Me ~

We can find it quite challenging to distinguish the difference between what is genuinely good and what is good for our selfish needs and desires. Although an innate knowledge of goodness exists within every person, the reality is that many of us struggle to find it because personal views and opinions easily become self-serving and conditional. By selfishly caring for our individual physical, spiritual, material, and emotional needs, we can forget or even intentionally ignore the fact that others require fulfillment of their own.

When a person perceives life in a self-centered way, negative thoughts and behaviors are often the unwelcome result. Examples of this negativity can range in severity from:

➢ Caring exclusively for one's needs;
➢ Believing one particular belief, view, or perspective is exclusively correct;
➢ Having such a selfish mindset that separation, violence, and theft seem justifiable.

Some people seem to find it increasingly difficult to be tolerant of lifestyles or views outside of their own inner circle. In today's world, perhaps more than ever, selfishness, ignorance, and intolerance can cause us to believe that our own experience of life, such as a certain spiritual belief, racial group, nationality, or culture is superior. Any differences, no matter how innocent or benign, can become objects of intolerance.

If we choose to ignore the fact that living with goodness benefits everyone, we will continue on a downward spiral of negativity and selfishness. The problem runs the gamut

7

from countries waging war to people committing crimes and violence to the smaller, selfish interactions of people on an individual basis. Even something as seemingly insignificant as cutting in front of someone in line, giving a rude gesture while driving, or making fun of someone detracts from goodness in the same way, although not to the same degree, as more selfish, violent, or immoral actions.

~ Negativity Detracts ~

With a negative perspective, you may believe that the concept of getting back to good is made up of nothing more than "pie in the sky" dreams or idealistic clichés that are too vague to put into action in a practical or effective way. You can easily rationalize that life is so hard, demanding, and unfair that spending time caring for your needs and desires can leave little time or ambition for you to be kind, giving, and selfless to someone or something else.

A negative outlook will allow you to believe the following statements:

➢ The world will not change for the better simply because a person volunteers time, donates money, or becomes more tolerant.

➢ Gestures of kindness and forgiveness will not make a difference.

➢ Bringing a meaningful, practical, positive change by thinking and acting with goodness is the stuff of fairy tales and not a part of the "real world."

➢ Lofty ideals look impressive on the written page, yet are not realistic when applied to the world in which we live.

➢ Getting back to good will not eliminate evil or hatred, so why bother.

****

Now that some negativity is out of the way, we can get on with our most important work.

****

While it may be true that changing small things in your everyday actions will not instantly bring about world peace or end world hunger, living with good thoughts and actions are as necessary to your life as air. To dismiss that fact by thinking you cannot make a difference is an easy submission, but *all* thoughts and behaviors that are good make a positive difference. In order to bring about constructive change, you must confront negative thoughts and actions by addressing and eliminating them to the greatest possible degree.

When we bring excessive complexity and selfishness to beliefs or ideas by focusing on processes, complicated rules, and "overly analyzed" interpretations, rather than focusing our time, resources, and energies on living with goodness, we are in effect choosing to move away from it. One excellent example of this is the approach that many people take toward spiritual beliefs or ideologies. Essentially, those beliefs have fundamental similarities and serve as guides to bring people closer to true goodness. However, when these beliefs and perspectives are narrowly focused and selfishly interpreted, the opposite occurs—they lead away from it. When this happens, we minimize and ignore the profound simplicity that resides within true faith, which is meant to foster and nurture the encouraging, beneficial aspects of life.

~ Find Your Way Back to Good ~

Come to understand, with an open mind, that there is a greater purpose for life than simply caring for the needs of you and yours. You are here to offer goodness toward others and toward nature, as well. As an individual with unique views and styles, you must find and develop your path back to good on your own terms with your own personal beliefs and values. The specific interpretation and implementation is for you to decide upon and incorporate in your own way; however, be careful not to concentrate on your interpretations so intensely that you forget to implement them.

You can get back to good by giving thankfulness, patience, material support, and kindness. Overcome intolerance, learn to replace selfishness with selflessness, and strive to treat others with respect and kindness in every aspect of life. Give to people you know, as well as to those you don't. Learn to give to your planet in your everyday routines. Apply goodness to yourself, to your family, to your relationships, and to your spiritual beliefs.

If great change does not happen immediately in your life, it does not mean the journey back to good will be fruitless. This journey requires consistency and time. Take small, constant steps and changes will come. As your thoughts, perspectives, and actions change, you will also see the people and world around you change. You can make a difference by affecting the lives of others positively. By taking part in this effort you are directly responsible for bringing more goodness into our world (one of the six billion ways). The ability to bring a great, sweeping change is literally within *your* power. This life can be better, and this world *will* be better, when you become as good as you can be.

"How lovely to think that no one need wait a moment, we can start now, start slowly changing the world. How lovely that everyone, great and small, can make their contribution...how we can always, always give something, if only kindness."
—Anne Frank

CHAPTER 2

Getting Back to Good
The Process.

*It is not what they profess, but what
they practice that makes them good.*
—Greek Proverb

Getting back to good is a process that makes living with goodness a priority. In order to accomplish this task, many different facets and aspects of life have to be individually and uniquely learned, worked through, and put into practice. This is not as simple as saying, "Practice what you preach," or "Just be good." Human beings are very complex creatures. We experience different situations and circumstances that constantly shape and mold the way we choose to think and act.

While basic rules of goodness are "programmed" in every human brain, they can only be applied by choice and effort. Much like a muscle, this inherent knowledge must be used often in order to keep it functional and strong. When a muscle is not used it becomes weak, frail, susceptible to damage, and unable to function properly. Similarly, when people do not choose to apply their inherent knowledge, that sense becomes weak and unable to function as designed, giving way to negativity and selfishness.

We must *choose* to live with goodness. To guide that choice, some people follow spiritual and religious doctrine while others may rely on a combination of other reasons. No matter what reason is given, the underlying purpose is fundamentally similar—the shared responsibility to follow our innate knowledge of goodness. Unfortunately, this inherent knowledge can be negatively affected by experiences and situations that can damage the ability to perceive what is truly good. When this occurs, we can lose sight of the fact that we are equal and commonly responsible for treating one another, as well as nature, with respect and selflessness— with the "Golden Rule" concept that is shared by all true beliefs.

While getting back to good may be difficult at times, it is certainly achievable. The basic elements and principles it emphasizes are straightforward and universal. Do not complicate them with unimportant, unnecessary details, complex guidelines, or principles of segregation and superiority; to do so only feeds negativity.

****

A key factor in getting back to good is to encourage the inherent knowledge of goodness within, and embrace that knowledge by choosing to follow through with positive thoughts and actions.

****

The following points serve as guides to get Back to Good:

1) Have faith in SomeThing Greater.
2) Connect with SomeThing Greater—connect with goodness. Find the path that is right for you.
3) Be tolerant and respectful of the countless views of spirituality that exist. Every person will have a unique view (even having no spiritual belief is a unique view) and must work to be tolerant of different outlooks and beliefs.

13

4) Give thanks every day for all that comes into your life, both good and (seemingly) bad.

5) Accept the fact that by nature, you are selfish to a degree, but also acknowledge that you maintain excessive selfishness by choice.

6) Look within to change. Identify and reduce selfishness by working to incorporate selfless thoughts and actions into your life.

7) Give to get back to good. Give help, patience, tolerance, and kindness; give forgiveness, love, and care for others. Foster goodness by giving as much as possible; nothing is too big or too small.

8) Take care of your physical, emotional, and spiritual health. You must feel good about yourself in order to help others to the best of your ability.

9) Find complete purpose for life by caring for your needs and giving to others.

10) Be good. Continually foster as much goodness as possible in your life. Accept the fact that there will be times when you may falter, but always work to find your way back to good.

~ SomeThing Greater ~

Humanity has wrestled with the mysteries surrounding existence since the beginning of time. Nature is such a miracle that many people believe it was Created. Conversely, others contend that science will eventually discover methods and procedures that can ultimately explain why and how everything has come into existence, from space to nature to life itself. Yet the inexplicable complexity and beauty of nature, which remains considerably beyond humanity's ability to understand, etches burning questions deep into the human psyche regarding meaning, purpose, and life itself.

Out of the dark, often incomprehensible reality that comprises our world, a vast majority of humanity strives to illuminate and bring meaning to life with faith in SomeThing Greater. Various ways of connecting to SomeThing beyond human perception and comprehension have spawned differing names, concepts, and beliefs that reflect the vast and varied social, cultural and personal differences of humanity. Some of those names and concepts include God (in any language), Spirit, Lord, Supreme Being, Higher Power, Creator, Karma, Light, Universal Energy, and Goodness; as well as countless other names and concepts that express unique views and perceptions of who and/or what "SomeThing Greater" encompasses. These views exist in many organized as well as individual ideas and beliefs.

****

In order to simplify the reading, God and SomeThing Greater will be the names used throughout the book. If these are not terms with which you're comfortable, then please use names and concepts you deem appropriate.

****

For our purposes here, any and all differing views of SomeThing Greater fit into our definition as long as true goodness remains. There will be no debates, rationalizations, or cases made concerning specific spiritual beliefs or views, because spirituality is largely a matter of personal faith, belief, spiritual opinion, and life experience.

****

Many people share the fundamental belief that God exists. Others contend that such a belief is not necessary in today's world because of scientific advances. Without getting into a debate of religion versus science, two conclusions can be drawn regarding existence.

The first conclusion is the belief that God is responsible in some way for existence. This view can be expressed through spirituality, religion, or a personal point of view. Ideally, these spiritual, religious, and personal views form a foundation of guiding principles by which to live and connect with goodness, as well as guides for people to be humble before nature and recognize humanity's place in the grand scheme.

The second conclusion is that everything has simply always existed. This view shuns any belief or acknowledgement of SomeThing Greater. Science and technology have opened a vault of knowledge and understanding which leads some people to conclude that nature and all that it encompasses is simply a product of happenstance and probability. This perspective essentially states that humanity will eventually be able to answer all questions regarding existence by means of science, technology, and our intelligence, thereby negating the necessity of belief in SomeThing Greater.

~ Connect With Goodness ~

Finding a spiritual connection is an association to goodness that is the next step in the process of getting back to good. For many people, a true connection is accomplished through religious or spiritual beliefs, while others may have a personal connection in some individual form. More than six billion unique views and perspectives of SomeThing Greater exist because every person on the planet owns a unique, personal view. As such, there are at least six billion ways to establish a connection, as long as it contains goodness and tolerance.

The manner in which a person chooses to connect is an immensely personal choice, and every individual knows what feels right on a personal level. However, selfishness or ignorance can attempt to justify the conviction that one particular view is exclusively correct. Such thinking leads to intolerance of differing beliefs and outlooks. Remember, a spiritual connection is designed to foster goodness, selflessness, and tolerance, not to cause harm, separation, or narrow-mindedness. Ironically, a major portion of the prejudice, selfishness, and suffering that afflicts our world stems from self-interested connections to goodness.

The way you choose to express your beliefs creates many responsibilities. Some of the greatest of those responsibilities are to live with goodness and be tolerant of the various, diverse paths of spirituality. Different cultures and individuals have unique ways of believing and worshipping, just as you may. Become tolerant and open-minded of that fact. In the end, to believe and worship means very little if it is not connected with behavior that fosters goodness and the tolerance of differing views.

~ Give Thanks ~

After you find a spiritual connection to goodness, the next step in getting back to good is to be thankful for everything in life, no matter what comes your way. I admit that is easier said than done. True thankfulness allows an appreciation of the fact that everything in life is given and helps us stop taking things for granted. Many people never become fully aware of what they have received in life, and mere inconveniences or normal challenges somehow grow into problems, while true difficulties unnecessarily turn into disasters. At other times, people may take what they have been given for granted, and develop a sense of entitlement. They may only realize the significance of what they have received when tragedy strikes or is narrowly averted.

You may be discouraged with the turns your life has taken and instead of being thankful, perhaps you think, "Why, God?

Why me? Why do I have to suffer or struggle with this trouble when other people do not? It's not fair!" Perhaps when difficult situations confront you, you think, "Why does God allow bad things to happen? God can't exist with all of the trouble and suffering in the world!" Such perspectives must be changed by completely understanding, noticing, and appreciating the gifts you receive every day.

One positive way to deal with difficult or adverse circumstances is to maintain an attitude of gratitude. When you are truly grateful, you realize that many problems in life may not be problems at all, merely selfish perceptions. Learn to feel blessed for what you have, and remember why you have it. Do not feel entitled to anything from God, because everything in life is a gift, even the day itself.

~ Selfish to Selfless ~

Human beings are selfish by nature. To care for ourselves, our loved ones, and the things we hold dear, we must be selfish to a certain degree—that is a fact of life. The task of caring for that which is important and close to us is natural and normal, but we can mistakenly do it to an excessive degree—to the exclusion and neglect of others. As we care for individual needs, we may become excessively selfish, materialistic, or extreme in aspects of life, while choosing to ignore the fact that others have needs, as well.

Selfishness can spill over into areas of life where it doesn't belong. When we believe one way is the only correct way to accomplish a certain objective, problems tend to develop. By choosing to ignore the fact that others have needs that are just as important as our own, negativity inevitably creates emotions, attitudes, and actions that lead away from goodness. We may become mean, jealous, or spiteful of others because of selfishness. Intolerance of diverse lifestyles, beliefs, and physical differences allows ignorance and hatred to breed and continue to grow unchecked.

Getting back to good requires that selfish thoughts and actions be replaced with selflessness. This process requires time and effort and begins with the willingness to admit that you are selfish in some ways. Simply because you may have what you need to some degree, such as health, money, or success, you should not exist to care *solely* for that which is important to you. Look beyond self-service and learn to identify and shun selfishness by committing to embrace selflessness.

~ Give ~

A major component of getting back to good is to give selflessly to others. Thoughts and actions are the only things you truly "own" in this life. As such, they are essentially the only things you can really give to others. As the keeper of your kindness, your tolerance, your positive attitude of gratitude, and your patience, you have the responsibility to give those things. Share them often.

All ways of giving are connected, and each one matters. At heart, they are one and the same. When you give kindness, you are giving help. When you are tolerant, you are being kind. When you are patient and polite, you give help, kindness, and tolerance. There are literally billions of ways to give, and the extent or amount that you are able to give makes no difference; the important thing is *to give*.

The act of giving is a manner of putting selfless thoughts and aspirations directly into action. To give in the truest sense of the word, means to do so for the sake of giving goodness, not because you expect to get something in return. You give because you know in your heart that it is the right thing to do. If you have what you need, learn to define your purpose as more than simply existing and caring for you and yours. Choose to reach out and find a way to add value to your life and to the lives of others. Find a way to give.

~ Take Care ~

In order to promote goodness, you must put yourself first to a certain extent. Having some degree of physical, emotional, and spiritual health is necessary in order to offer goodness to your full potential. Feeling unhealthy affects outlooks and attitudes negatively and makes it more difficult for you to foster goodness. If you notice areas in your life that require attention, find effective ways to take care of them. While the responsibility to care for yourself is ultimately your own, you don't have to do it alone. Many avenues and resources are available to help improve every aspect of your well-being. Remember, a strong desire to get back to good is dramatically weakened if you do not take care of yourself.

~ Find Meaning — Life's Purpose ~

Have you ever felt that you are missing something in life or constantly searching for something more? Human beings instinctively search for meaning and purpose, and this need must be satisfied in many different ways in order for you to feel complete. You may succeed in a career, raise a family, or accomplish your goals and dreams, but still you cannot realize a complete purpose for life unless you actively seek to live with true goodness.

Many of us make the mistake of becoming so involved with the search for purpose that we look right past or through the reasons for it. We can lose sight of life's meaning when we become overly focused on our wants, our needs, and our lives. To put it in simple terms: *We can find complete purpose for life by achieving our goals and dreams while connecting with, and fostering true goodness.* Yes, it is that simple. The rules are already written; the intuition is already there.

~ **Start Your Journey** ~

Getting back to good is a journey where you will find marvelous scenery and learn many wonderful lessons. You will experience a genuine, tangible feeling for life. By choosing to maintain a positive perspective, an attitude of gratitude, and a commitment to be a giving person, you will encourage selflessness and goodness in your life.

This journey can be tough and there will be times when you lose sight of your destination. Whenever that happens, find your way back to thoughts and actions of goodness. No matter what happened in the past, you can benefit by making a change now. The particular ways to travel back to good are for you to decide. Your beliefs, views, and individual distinctions are unique and special to you, playing a large part in how you address *your* responsibility. Find your path back to good.

CHAPTER 3

The Tie That Binds
SomeThing Greater — Believe

*"Science is not only compatible with
spirituality, it is a profound source of spirituality."*
—Carl Sagan

The first step on the journey back to good is to have faith
in SomeThing Greater; SomeThing beyond human perception
and comprehension. This is a foundation for living with
goodness. Many people are questioning the need to believe
in God and seem to find it increasingly difficult to maintain
such a belief. Others reject such an existence entirely due
to scientific discovery, human ingenuity, and technological
advances.

If you do not believe in God, or if you find yourself on
the fence about such a belief, contemplate the simplicity of
our most complex scientific findings and formulae. Scientific
theories and procedures, as they get more accurate, precise,
and complex, actually provide subtle, powerful evidence for
the existence of SomeThing Greater at a fundamental level.

People who have faith through spiritual, religious, and
personal beliefs may not require evidence to validate those
beliefs, and may find Chapters 3 and 4 somewhat redundant
or unnecessary. However, everyone could benefit from
understanding that spiritual belief is not meant to separate
or exclude, but to transform spiritual knowledge and faith
into thoughts and actions of true goodness.

Many people strive to create meaning with belief in SomeThing Greater than themselves. Various ways and means of connecting to SomeThing beyond human perception and comprehension have spawned differing concepts and beliefs that reflect the vast and varied experience of humanity. As I have said before, these ideas are fundamentally important to our work of getting back to good, as long as the basis of the belief is true goodness.

~ Past Beliefs of Humanity ~

Throughout history human beings have formed numerous beliefs and views regarding SomeThing Greater. Individuals, cultures, and entire civilizations have spent vast amounts of time exploring differing spiritual views. We can prove this by noting the formation of various religions and belief systems, and the magnificent structures dedicated to worship. Enormous amounts of energy and ingenuity were used to show reverence, awe, and humility.

We can surely argue that the reason our ancestors believed so strongly in SomeThing Greater is because they lacked the degree of scientific knowledge and information to which we are privy today. Belief systems were structured on and around physical events and occurrences within nature and the human body. Ancient peoples did not comprehend the physical forces that caused earthquakes, volcanoes, and other natural disasters, or the weather patterns that created terrible storms. When a devastating physical event occurred, they believed that God(s) had become angry. Our ancestors had no knowledge of what the sun, moon, and stars really were, and droughts, diseases, and epidemics were taken as signs of a deity's unhappiness. They didn't understand the physical reasons for illness. Only a belief in SomeThing Greater could explain the unknown.

23

~ **Humanity Comes of Age with Science** ~

Science brings a huge volume of facts and comprehension into the realm of human knowledge. It is only in the relatively recent past — 300 years or so — that modern scientific principles have ushered in mechanical and industrial revolutions. Most familiar to us is the immediate past of the 20th Century when we achieved more scientific progress than ever before. Technological advances have allowed us to travel off Mother Earth, clone living beings, split atoms, map the human genome, and use computer technology to create the current informational revolution.

As a species, we have never had the scientific ability to understand the functioning of nature or life to the degree we do today. Our current level of understanding begins to afford us a deeper insight into how nature functions and we now understand why volcanic eruptions, earthquakes, and catastrophic storms occur. Through science, we have proven the existence of natural laws which fundamentally govern all procedures in the physical universe. Or so we think.

With respect to living things, we know more clearly how life functions. The basic coding of genetics has been deciphered to show that life follows a type of "programming." Complex chemical reactions carry out these programmed instructions in precise order, causing inanimate particles to coalesce in such a way as to produce life. Overall, we have a better understanding of how organisms live, die, repair, and survive. We can fight off many diseases, and understand that microscopic organisms, genetic abnormalities, and other natural influences are underlying causes for sickness and illness.

Scientific findings have opened our eyes to the profound complexity and intricacy of nature, allowing us to disprove many theories and ideas of old, and change perceptions of what may have once been considered achievable only by God. By constantly learning more of what was previously unknown, we now have answers to many of the questions and uncertainties of the past. Granted, we have only scratched the surface of scientific discovery, but we understand enough about life to know that it is impossibly complex.

~ Views of Creation Change ~

As science and technology progress, the amount of knowledge gained leads many people to believe that there are logical, scientific explanations for existence. With all of the information that has been discovered, learned, and theorized, we can easily come to engage in a type of scientific arrogance. This arrogance causes people to rationalize that there may be no need to believe in God, and contends that science will be able to decode the mysteries of nature through tangible, quantitative, and qualitative facts. We can come to believe that human beings will eventually be able to comprehend everything there is to know.

To think science will be able to find the answer to many questions and subjects is not a bad notion, but to think it will be able to uncover answers regarding meaning and existence creates a climate of unhealthy expectation. Although we become more advanced and prolific in every scientific field on a daily basis, the knowledge we gain can provide a false sense of empowerment and confidence. We often forget just how small and insignificant we are when compared to the natural world that sustains us. Forgetting where we have come from and why we are allowed to continue, causes haughty misperceptions, ideas, and behaviors that lead us away from goodness and humility — a very dangerous path to follow.

~Where Did Everything Come From? ~

Our universe is a vast, inconceivably complex structure. The beauty, power, and awe-inspiring magnificence of nature overwhelms the senses. We are at a loss to describe its complexity whether we are looking at the night sky through the world's most powerful telescope or at the fascinating aspects of life under a microscope.

Setting aside spiritual beliefs and scientific views, the bottom line is that nature and life exist. From the billions of people on Earth to the millions of forms of life on our planet, from the depths of the oceans to the tiny specks of light from distant stars and galaxies that are visible in the night sky, physically, nature and life are evident — they exist. Therefore, two possible conclusions can be drawn concerning that existence. The first conclusion is that SomeThing created (not necessarily in a particular religious sense) everything. The second conclusion is that our universe has simply always existed.

****

The following is an admittedly elementary explanation addressing fundamental facts that do not require detailed information to support the concepts. In fact, the more complex our scientific information becomes, the more fundamental evidence presents itself for the existence of SomeThing Greater.

****

If, after gazing into the heavens and at the natural world around you, you do not believe SomeThing beyond our comprehension is responsible for our physical universe, then reflect for a moment as to where you are right now — not where you are in life, but where you are physically. What are you standing on? What are you sitting on? What is supporting you? There is, in fact, some sort of matter and energy below you or around you. Whether you are jumping out of a plane or snuggling up on the couch, you are touching matter and experiencing energy as one element or another, in one form or another.

Matter/energy contains the building blocks of the universe, forming stars, planets, and ultimately, life. These building blocks physically exist; we can touch them, see them, experiment with them, and use them — they are real. Since matter/energy physically exists, there must be an explanation for how it came into being. Where did it come from? Let's explore our two options.

1. Matter/energy (ultimately life) has always existed.

Or

2. SomeThing created matter/energy (ultimately life); SomeThing that humanity is not able to comprehend from our limited perspective, experience, and ability.

****

No matter which scientific, religious, or spiritual view is taken, these are two absolute possibilities that can explain existence.

****

~What is more likely? ~

Logic and science dictate that physical events do not just happen. There is always cause and effect. Conservation Laws (i.e. The Law of Conservation of Mass) dictate matter/energy cannot be physically created or destroyed (from our limited understanding); therefore it could not have always existed since there is no cause to that effect. Even though science thoroughly explains how nature works, by proving the existence of natural laws and various theories, physical procedures, and processes, it is limited to exactly that — understanding *how* nature works.

While science can surely decipher many aspects of nature's complex puzzle, it cannot completely decode the enigma of existence or the authority of natural laws (a law by definition must be given authority by SomeThing). Consequently, choice number one is ruled out. This may seem like an over-simplified or speculative statement, but the truth ultimately resides in simplicity.

No matter how complex or advanced scientific knowledge becomes, there will always be at least two questions that cannot be answered scientifically: "Where did everything come from?" and, "What retains authority over natural laws?" The answer is clear if you *choose* to see it: SomeThing Greater. Granted, this requires a leap of faith, but searching for this answer can be so complex that the simplicity of its truth can be overlooked quite easily. After all, is the existence of God more improbable than our own?

~ A Matter of Fact — A Matter of Faith ~

The facts are there, and you have the prerogative to interpret those facts in your own way. You may choose to believe in the existence of God or in theories that try to disprove such an existence, but either choice requires faith. You can choose to have faith in SomeThing Greater or you can choose to have faith in randomness, nothingness, and happenstance. Ultimately that choice is yours, but choosing to have faith in God is a faith in SomeThing Greater than oneself — SomeThing more than the here and now.

Faith in God does not require one to denounce science or forsake it. On the contrary, it accepts that scientific facts and theories help us understand life by explaining the "how" of nature — not the "why" of nature. Theories, beliefs, and opinions can be argued *ad infinitum* on this subject, but the belief in God should be stronger now than ever — because of science, not in spite of it.

****

Discussions regarding science, first cause, scientific theory, and spiritual/religious views of creation are beyond the scope of this book. For a more in-depth look into those matters, I am currently working on a book entitled, Crealution.

****

Ultimately, simple absolutes provide evidence for the existence of SomeThing Greater at a most fundamental level, which is the common thread categorically tying humanity together. It ties you to me, and both of us to every person on the planet. Most importantly, it weaves humanity into the garment of nature — SomeThing that is common to all.

Bickering about which scientific theory or spiritual belief is exclusively correct is futile. Instead, have faith by acknowledging that SomeThing Greater exists in whatever way you see fit and spend your energy on the more creative, helpful pursuits of humanity. No matter what your opinions and beliefs are, one of the most important things you can do is to have faith in SomeThing Greater.

~ Connect with SomeThing Greater ~
Connect with Goodness

The choice to have faith is one you are free to make. However, true faith means more than simply acknowledging that God exists. It means understanding and accepting that goodness is a part of God and that you must find a meaningful, selfless connection to that goodness. When you choose to have faith, you are choosing to accept a responsibility to live with goodness in thought as well as action. Without it, there cannot be a complete or true connection.

Learn to perceive the design of goodness that is within you and in the nature that surrounds you. Remember, humanity ultimately stems from true goodness and is responsible for fostering it. Find *your* connection in a religious, spiritual, or personal way.

"Science can purify religion from error and superstition. Religion can purify science from idolatry and false absolutes."
—Pope John Paul II

✓ To Do List: The Tie That Binds — Believe

❑ **Have faith in SomeThing Greater.**

❑ **Accept that science explains the "how" of nature, not the "why" of nature:**
—Science can decipher and explain processes and procedures.
—Science cannot explain what gives natural laws authority, nor will it be able to fully account for the origins of existence.

❑ **Find a tolerant, genuine connection to goodness.**

❑ **Use your faith as a path to goodness.**

<u>Notes:</u>

CHAPTER 4

Connect With Goodness
Find your connection.

*The function of prayer is not to influence God,
but rather to change the nature of the one who prays.*
—Kierkegaard

A spiritual connection is an association to goodness that lends stability and purpose to life, directs you toward a path of righteousness, and exists through your thoughts and actions. Your connection can be personal, religious, spiritual, or in another form or combination that works for you.

Differing spiritual views form the basis of the countless belief systems, religions, and personal beliefs that exist throughout the world. No matter which path you choose, there are equally important facts that apply. You create a true spiritual connection through beliefs *and* thoughts and actions of goodness. No true spiritual teachings advocate intolerance or harm, especially in the name of spiritual principles. Connecting to God means you are choosing to accept the responsibility of living with goodness. Establish and strengthen your connection to the goodness that is God.

Spiritual belief is one of the most comforting aspects of life. It can provide support and understanding through the different situations and challenges we face. In addition, spirituality can bring great joy, peace of mind, and meaning to life. Most importantly, a spiritual connection helps foster goodness toward yourself, your loved ones, those you may not personally know, and to the natural world around you.

****

When we reflect on the magnificence of our reality and the profound experiences we are capable of, the inherent knowledge of SomeThing Greater becomes evident. A major purpose of spirituality is to guide us to live with goodness by being thankful, kind, respectful, and tolerant of one another.

****

~ Spiritual Instincts ~

From ancient cultures to modern-day belief systems, humanity has demonstrated an instinctual connection to God. Deep in the human psyche is a connection to SomeThing that is responsible for the beauty and complexity that surrounds and encompasses us. This connection innately guides us to goodness.

We are hard-wired with survival instincts in order to maintain physical life. At the same time, we are wired with instincts to help us find spirituality. These instincts give us the inherent knowledge that SomeThing Greater exists and that we must achieve a spiritual connection. The blueprints for goodness, if you will, are already in place. What you build from those blueprints is up to you.

How can a person bridge the gap from knowing that God exists to finding a true connection to goodness? Fortunately, the primary connection is already present with our spiritual instincts, but the influence these instincts can exert is limited because they only serve as guides to goodness. Ultimately, you are responsible for using your instincts to make the choice to have faith and exemplify a true connection.

~ Find Your Path ~

More than six billion individual beliefs and views of spirituality exist throughout humanity. Every person owns a unique spiritual opinion and outlook. Often, people relate to spirituality by directing their belief into something tangible and belief systems frequently become the avenue they follow to that end. While some spiritual beliefs remain completely personal, others are organized through major religions; however, every true belief can be a unique way to connect with God.

All true beliefs share basic tenets of goodness that are fundamentally similar — to have faith, to act with goodness and humility, to be thankful, selfless, kind, and tolerant (the Ethic of Reciprocity or Golden-Rule concept that is common to every true belief). Of course, specific views, practices, and fixed doctrines differentiate various beliefs, but all true beliefs share an equal place in our world when they are carried out with goodness.

Seek out spirituality, and find a connection that is right for you. Only you truly know what spiritual bond feels right. You will know you have achieved a true spiritual connection when you connect to God by living with thoughts and actions of goodness. Remember, no true connection will cause or encourage intolerance, indifference, or violence, even to the smallest degree.

~ Focus On the True Message ~

Learn to balance the needs and requirements of your spiritual beliefs with thoughts and actions of goodness. Concentrate on being thankful, practicing your faith in earnest, acting kindly, and reaching out to others. If you are more worried about obtaining artifacts or visiting places associated with your beliefs than with offering goodness, you are doing your faith an injustice. Spiritual beliefs ultimately exist to connect with God and promote goodness.

Many belief systems have some or all of the following characteristics:

➢ A storied history with holy places or locations,
➢ Distinct rituals and artifacts,
➢ Holy texts,
➢ Fixed doctrines and moral codes.

These things are an immensely important part of spiritual belief, and can give a tangible aspect to faith that helps followers understand abstract concepts that may be difficult to comprehend. However, people can focus too intensely on the material aspects of faith while not giving the appropriate amount of attention to core teachings of goodness.

Do not discount the importance of the customs, places, and items of a particular belief, as those things help validate that belief for what it is, what it stands for, and where it came from. However, there must be a balance between practicing the belief and living with goodness. If you place too much emphasis on places, rituals, or words, while neglecting to live with goodness, you obscure the fundamental reasons for faith. As important as material aspects and specific practices are to a particular belief, they are merely tools to help you think about, reflect on, and accomplish what a true belief is teaching — a connection to goodness. Do not become so involved with the material aspects of spiritual beliefs that you lose your focus on fundamental teachings of goodness.

~ Many Ways to Connect ~

Spiritual beliefs come in many styles and shapes, and are fundamentally similar in that they share universal ideas and guidelines. Although differing beliefs may vary in specific expressions of faith, in the end they ultimately serve the same purpose. With the various types of religious/spiritual beliefs and perspectives throughout the world, and the many different views and interpretations within each one, which single belief or perspective is exclusively correct? While no one true belief is *solely* right to the exclusion of all others, beliefs that teach of SomeThing Greater and living with goodness can be true and equal. To argue one creed or belief as solely correct defeats the purpose of faith and becomes a useless argument that no one can definitively win. Remember, a true connection does not teach or condone intolerance.

****

If you do not share the perspective that different paths connect with God, then agree to disagree on that point without being disagreeable. Remember instead to concentrate on your responsibility for goodness. Continue to become a more tolerant person in every aspect of life, especially spiritually, and always work to find more ways to live with goodness.

****

Learn to look beyond personal prejudice or bias toward different beliefs and creeds by acknowledging the goodness that all true beliefs share. Ultimately, you will choose a spiritual connection that feels right and works for you. Please give others the freedom to do the same. Remember, God is the tie that binds. Spiritual interpretations that are laced with intolerance break that binding tie.

****

~ **Spiritual Tolerance** ~

The greatest problems with respect to spiritual beliefs are the disagreements that people can have concerning varying religious or spiritual outlooks. Spirituality is a very personal and deep-rooted aspect of life, and spiritual convictions are often so strong and profound that tolerating and respecting different views can be very difficult for some people. Nevertheless, living with goodness dictates that we become as tolerant as possible in every aspect of our existence, especially concerning religious and spiritual beliefs.

Some people may have trouble accepting the fact that there can be more than one way to have faith in God. However, just as there is more than one correct way for people to communicate, more than one way to set up governments, and more than one way to put up a fence, there is more than one way to interpret our spiritual instincts through different religious and spiritual beliefs. If you maintain the conviction that only your way of thinking can bring you to God, your spiritual views can become selfishly skewed. Problems begin when people try to force their own convictions onto others. If you think that one particular view is superior to all others, faith can be soured with intolerance and separation, and you can lose the fundamental tenets of spirituality. Intolerance of differing true beliefs ultimately leads away from goodness. (See Chapter 9 for a detailed look at this topic.)

If you do not know about differing beliefs, or do not feel completely comfortable with other spiritual customs and perspectives, remember that spiritual tolerance does not ask you to believe or worship in a different way. Spiritual tolerance only asks that you become open to the fact that more than one way can connect with God. You are doing no disservice to your faith by being tolerant of other true beliefs or religions.

On the contrary, being tolerant is an act of goodness that true faith expects and requires from you.

****

It is the apex of hypocrisy to claim to be spiritually connected, but to live at the same time without spiritual tolerance. Intolerance of differing true beliefs or perspectives felt inwardly or expressed outwardly is contradictory to the tenets of true spirituality.

****

Spiritual faith can fill a person with joy and happiness. Many people feel the need to express that fulfillment by telling others about it, which is completely normal and good. Extend goodness and helpfulness through your beliefs, instead of trying to justify why a certain belief is the exclusive, solitary connection. The task of fostering goodness in life is far more important than arguing about which belief is the only right one.

The manner in which you express spirituality is a personal choice. As long as you maintain true faith and live with goodness, you are headed in the right direction. Since you know what a proper, comfortable connection feels like for yourself, please extend that same freedom of choice to others. Once you are tolerant of differing beliefs and perspectives, tolerance seems effortless in other aspects of life. Focus your energy on what truly matters — a spiritual connection that fosters goodness.

****

Spirituality is only as important as how it leads to living with goodness and tolerance. No matter whether you maintain spiritual faith with a Monotheistic, Polytheistic,

Karmic, or Pantheistic view, or favor a philosophy such as agnosticism, secular humanism or atheism instead, one truth remains for all: GOODNESS. We must strive to live with goodness.

****

~ Connect With Goodness ~

Even though much of humanity professes to have faith in SomeThing Greater, and countless houses of worship practice beliefs that instruct followers to live with goodness, the unfortunate reality is that many of those teachings may not make it out the front door to become thoughts and actions of goodness in the world. Similarly, the fundamental instructions of goodness that are the inspired word of many holy texts read by billions of people of differing beliefs often do not make it off the written page to become thoughts and actions of goodness. Instead, spiritual beliefs are selfishly incorporated into personal needs, wants, and desires.

****

If humanity put half of the energy and effort it spends disagreeing about which belief is exclusively right, into practicing goodness instead, the world would be back to good.

****

Your *choice* to have faith is free and personal. The manner in which you make that connection is unique and individual. Somewhere along the way we seem to have lost sight of the fact that when choosing to believe in God, we must also think and act with goodness. That is not a choice. Find a true connection to the goodness that is God.

Here in the maddening

maze of things,

When tossed by storm and flood:

To one fixed ground my

spirit clings,

I know that God is Good...

—*John G. Whittier*

✓ ## To Do List: Connect With Goodness

❑ **Fulfill your instinctual need to connect to SomeThing Greater.**

❑ **Realize the purpose of spirituality:**
—Connect to God with goodness.
—Focus on being thankful.
—Think and act with selflessness.
—Believe in Something Greater than humankind (and yourself).

❑ **Connect with goodness:**
—Choose the responsibility to act with goodness.
—Do not cause harm, be intolerant, act selfishly, or foster hatred, *especially* in the name of a spiritual belief.
—Negotiate any perceived problems in life with the courage a spiritual connection provides.

❑ **Focus on the true message of your connection:**
—Focus on being thankful, practicing your faith in earnest, acting kindly, and living with tolerance.
—Do not focus on the material aspects and specific practices of a spiritual belief to the point where you are not promoting goodness.

❑ **Become open to accepting that differing true beliefs are able connect with God:**
—Recognize that humanity, by nature, requires many differing spiritual views.
—Accept that more than one particular belief or view can connect with God.

—Understand that different religions, belief systems, and personal views of spirituality come in many styles, shapes, and sizes, in order to fit the differing needs and circumstances of humanity.

❑ **Become tolerant of differing spiritual views.**

—Foster goodness instead of proclaiming a particular spiritual belief as the only way to God.

—Illuminate the basic meaning of faith by showing tolerance of all true beliefs.

—Learn about and respect different true beliefs to avoid spiritual tunnel vision.

Notes:

CHAPTER 5

Look Up — Be Thankful

Maintain trusting faith and thankfulness for the good and bad in your life.

"Gratitude is not only the greatest of virtues, but the parent of all the others."
—Marcus Tullius Cicero

After you have established a spiritual connection, the next step in getting back to good is to strengthen your perspective of thankfulness. Most of us know that saying thank you for things we receive is the right thing to do. We offer thanks to others for holding the door open, for helping us through tough situations, and for giving us gifts. Many times, however, we forget to say thank you or do not feel thankful for what we have received from God.

Thankfulness is a perspective that encompasses every aspect of life. It is more than simply saying thank you in a prayer or with a thought. It must be shown with actions. When you take something for granted, become mad at God, or ask, "Why me?" you are failing to be thankful. If you cause harm or act selfishly, you are not being grateful. Incorporate an attitude of gratitude into your life with your thoughts and through your actions.

Try not to complain, feel mad, or become sad when facing challenging situations. Granted, this may be difficult to do and it will take time to learn how to put into action; but a perspective of thankfulness allows you to better tolerate adversity and realize that nothing can be taken from you because nothing is truly yours. Always try to find something to be grateful for in life. Look up — be thankful.

Thankfulness is a matter of perspective. With it you can find happiness and peace of mind no matter what challenges come your way. Without it you can become unhappy or despondent with life even if you have a great state of affairs. Feeling grateful when all is going well is relatively easy, but when adversity strikes, *losing* an outlook of gratitude and being quick to ask, "Why God? Why me?" can be just as easy.

~ The Foundation of Thankfulness ~

In order for you to achieve and maintain a thankful outlook, you must strengthen views that support your foundation of thankfulness and remove obstacles that chip and rot it away. No one can force you to feel grateful or make you see the goodness and positive things that exist in your life. That point of view must come from you.

Remember and strengthen these thankful views:
1. Be thankful to God.
2. Be thankful for each day.
3. Be thankful for your health.
4. Be thankful for your abilities.

Remove these obstacles toward thankfulness:
1. Taking things for granted.
2. Feeling entitled.
3. Dealing with tough, tragic times without a thankful perspective.

47

4. Pitying yourself because of your problems.

5. Worrying about situations you have no control over.

Use these tips to maintain your thankful perspective:

1. A thankful checklist.

2. That's life!

3. Thankfulness can be achieved.

~ Strengthen Thankful Views ~

Use the following sections to learn how to uphold a thankful perspective. Although it may not be possible to feel genuinely grateful all of the time, honestly putting these insights into practice will help you feel thankful more often without having to give it a second thought.

1: Thank God

The foundation of a thankful perspective starts with giving thanks to God every day for everything in your life. Thanking God is the foundation that leads to a life without problems, struggles, or hardship. This is not to say that you won't experience tough, troubling, or challenging situations, because everyone does; however, genuinely thanking God gives you a positive perspective that can combat the negative effects of adversity and allow you to focus on the big picture.

Always be mindful of the fact that everything in life is given to you — even the day itself. Sure, you may own things on paper or have your name associated with achievements, titles, or positions, but ultimately you only have such things because they have been given to you. Thank God every day with your thoughts *and* through your actions of goodness.

2: Be Thankful For Each New Day

Feel grateful for each new day. Apply this gratefulness on a global scale as well as to your personal life. While you must be personally thankful for waking each day and for what is in your life, it is equally important to remember that humankind collectively receives a gift with every new sunrise. The possibility exists that some type of celestial or natural event, such as a meteor impact, a super-volcanic eruption, or other Earth-ending disaster could befall our planet and totally annihilate life as we know it. Granted, the odds of such an event are ridiculously small, but the possibility does exist. And there is always the more realistic possibility of the hundreds of different, "smaller" natural disasters that could throw our lives into chaos at any time around the neighborhood or around the world. These scenarios are not written to scare you or proclaim that the end is near, but to help you remember how small the human race is in the overall scheme of existence.

We have invented, discovered, and created many magnificent things, but they pale in comparison to the natural world. Our technological advancements and discoveries are insignificant when compared to the forces of nature, and overconfidence in humanity's power of technology can lead you to forget that our power is as fragile and feeble as life itself. Any human progress and achievement relies on the fact that we are given each new day. Our advancements would not be possible without the opportunities nature affords us.

Life exists on this planet only as long as the sun continues to shine and rain continues to fall. Thank God for each new day by acknowledging that every day is a gift and should not be taken for granted. Be humble and show thanks for the awesome power and splendor of nature by treating it with respect, which includes acting with goodness. When we are in awe of nature, we are really in awe of SomeThing Greater.

3: Be Thankful For Your Health

Once you have offered thanks for the dawning of each new day, be thankful for the health you have. The first step in doing so is recognizing that your health is not your own. It is a gift you receive. Of course, you are responsible for caring for yourself, but health is ultimately out of your control. Even if you maintain a healthy lifestyle, you can become afflicted with disease and disability. If you are not blessed with health in certain aspects of life you can be thankful for the areas in which you are healthy. By focusing gratitude on areas in life where you have been blessed, you can better deal with any difficulties that may affect you. Learn to work with the health you have and to be thankful for it.

Everything in nature is designed to have a limited existence, from the six hundred year old redwood tree to the three-day life cycle of a mosquito. Be mindful of the fact that age happens and illness occurs. Do not feel mad, sad, or cheated, as aging and illness are a natural part of life. They should not be feared or resented, and only become an issue when self-pity takes over. Self-pity rears its head when we start asking, "Why, God? Why me? Why do I have to suffer?" In truth, the question we should be asking is, "Why not me?"

Take action to correct and prevent health ailments where you have the ability to do so. If you are unable to remedy some issues you must learn how to accept that fact and be thankful for the health you *do* have — use it to promote goodness. Always remember to thank God every day for health because it can be taken in an instant!

4: Be Thankful For Ability

We often neglect to be thankful in recognizing the abilities God has given. In order to achieve your goals, you may have to sacrifice and work through difficult situations. Working diligently to accomplish your goals should give you a feeling of pride and a sense of ownership. Those feelings are normal and healthy, up to a certain point. You must put forth the effort, sacrifice, and work for your achievements, but the only reason you are able to accomplish them is because God has *given* you what you need to do so (i.e., the day itself, health, talents).

You are not being grateful if you feel too much pride in your abilities or achievements. An overabundance of pride or false pride leads to selfishness and negativity, which can cause you to believe you are better than someone else. When you feel superior in some way due to your abilities or accomplishments, you are not acting in a thankful manner.

How many people do you know who treat others poorly simply because they have differing degrees of material possessions, abilities, status, or achievements? If you recognize these behaviors in yourself, immediately take thankful action. Ground yourself to the fact that you are given what you need in order to achieve what you attain. Remember, you are equal to everyone no matter your status or pursuits in life.

Maintaining a thankful perspective means feeling blessed to be as smart, creative, and successful as you are. When you view your abilities as gifts, you will not feel superior or better than others. Instead you will treat others equally and with respect, no matter how their accomplishments, status, educational level, or social group differs from your own.

~ **Removing Obstacles** ~

To achieve and maintain thankfulness, you must reduce the obstacles that hinder an attitude of gratitude. The behaviors explained in the following segments hinder thankful perspectives. Learn to recognize when and where these behaviors appear in your life and work to remove them.

1: Taking For Granted

In order to enjoy the richness and fullness of life we must learn to stop taking things for granted. That phrase is very clichéd — only because it is so very correct! Human beings can be self-centered creatures who take many aspects of life for granted every day. It is easy to overlook the fact that everything we have, no matter how large or small, is a gift, however, once you truly realize what you have been given, you can naturally be abundantly thankful.

All too often, life is turned upside down in the blink of an eye by hardship or tragedy. Unfortunately, this is often the only time many people realize their blessings. Another cliché testifies to that fact: "You don't know what you've got until it's gone." The wisdom of these clichés is not to be ignored. You can agree with them now or be forced to accept them later.

In order to become more thankful, start with the simple act of thinking about what you have in front of you every day. Learn to recognize what you have been given and to be thankful for it. Make a list of all that you are grateful for and reflect on these gifts. Remember what you have — from your health, to your loved ones, to another day — and you will begin to achieve a more thankful attitude by *choosing* to take nothing for granted.

2: I'm Entitled To That!

When you take life for granted, a sense of entitlement frequently follows. You may believe that you are owed a nice, healthy, prosperous, and rewarding life. However, the truth is that you are not entitled to health, happiness, or even life from God. They are gifts. Always view them as such and be grateful for what you receive.

****

Transform any sense of entitlement into thankful actions of goodness.

****

Do you feel entitled rather than thankful? Have you reflected on the fact that the ability to live, achieve, and be successful is a *gift*? While you may be successful and achieve your goals, remember, you are *allowed* to do these things — not entitled to them. All of your accomplishments and abilities are not entirely your own, and they can be taken from you in an instant. While feeling proud and pleased about achievements and abilities is good, always remain thankful for the fact that you are given the ability to accomplish.

3: Tough Times — Tragic Times

Terrifying stories or occurrences of hardship, injury, tragedy, and death have touched every one of us in some way. We hear about them on the news, from people we know, or find out firsthand through personal experience. When tragedy strikes it can be shocking and horrifying. Unfortunately, this is often the only time our eyes are truly open to the reality of what belongs to us — *nothing*! No amount of money or perceived power can undo a tragic accident or death, control nature, or stop undesirable things from happening. These things are beyond our control.

During tough and tragic times, a selfish, thankless attitude causes you to feel slighted and treated unfairly. Those feelings, in turn, fuel a host of negative emotions and thoughts. I have often heard people exclaim, "How could God allow this to happen? I've been a good person. Why is this happening to me? There is no God, because God would not allow such awful things to happen!" When you find yourself asking these questions, you are not thinking thankfully. Coping with your challenges and troubles with an attitude of gratitude may be difficult, but try to remember all that you should be grateful for in order to ease your pain.

~ Conquer Difficult Situations ~

Tough, tragic times can be very difficult to cope with and many emotions come to the forefront to help you deal with the pain, confusion, and anger you may feel. These feelings are a normal part of the process of learning to cope. However, you can also apply positive thoughts, actions, and attitudes to create a thankful attitude that will lessen the severity and duration of any pain and suffering you may endure

Coping method 1: *Trust God.*

Trust God, even if you don't understand why bad things happen. Your spiritual connection, your attitude of gratitude, and your faith in goodness will help replace all pain with understanding in due time. How many times has something happened to you that seemed to be bad, only to turn out good in the end? Another cliché comes to mind: "a blessing in disguise."

Sometimes you may feel like there are no answers to your questions. Perhaps you will learn the reason for dire life events or hardships later in life, or even after life. Above all, learn to put your faith and trust in God and continue to live with goodness.

Coping method 2: *Accept the fact that adversity will strike.*

Adversity strikes during the course of every life. That is a fact. Loved ones are lost; family members, friends, and innocent people experience tragedy every day. Debilitating illnesses grab hold of people, forcefully squeezing and choking the life out of them. Forces of nature create havoc, tragic accidents occur, and chasms created by humankind seize life, health, and happiness. How can anyone effectively cope with such things?

One way to deal with adversity is to accept it as a natural part of life, in that difficulty and hardship will not always find someone else or happen to the "other person." When adversity appears in your life, find a way to effectively cope with it, and try to understand what you need to learn from it. Although it may seem impossible to find gratitude in some situations, you must confront adversity with the strength and positive attitude a thankful perspective provides.

Coping method 3: *Think of how any given situation could be worse.*

Try not to get caught up in the "Why me?" syndrome, which combines discouragement with self-pity. When facing tough times or hardship, you may feel horrible, helpless, and angry. **STOP!** Granted, these emotions and feelings are part of a process to help you deal with hardship and tragedy, but try to be thankful that your circumstances are only as bad as they are, because it could be worse.

Here's a trick to cope more effectively with tough times — visualize completely unbearable circumstances. Imagine that a loved one has suffered traumatic injuries in a terrible accident but she is still alive. Of course you may be scared and worried, and you probably feel terrible about seeing her in such a situation. But now, imagine that you lost your loved one in that accident. Think and reflect upon what that would be like. Dream in vivid detail about the memorial service, the lonely holidays, and the emptiness in your home. Click back to reality and be thankful for what you do have. This exercise has been completed correctly if you feel like you have just awakened from an awful nightmare, and now understand that your situation is not as bad as it could be.

When you can't imagine something worse...

Sometimes people face circumstances where they understandably cannot imagine anything worse. At this point, you must turn to faith. Remember, truly connecting to goodness means having faith and trusting God for *every* situation that crosses your path — not only during the good times.

When you suffer the loss of a loved one, remember to be grateful for what you have had with them. Remember the touch, the time, the smiles, and the love. *Do not forget those things.* At the very least, feel thankful and blessed for the time you were given with him or her. Do not forget that you were *given* time — that time was not yours.

Coping method 4: *Accept that dealing with adversity gets easier as time passes.*

To understand this coping method, it is necessary to look back at some occasion when you were in a great deal of physical pain. Perhaps you suffered an injury or had an operation. At the time, the pain may have felt unbearable, but somehow you lived through it and managed to deal with it. Now, try to remember how the physical pain felt. Can you recall the feeling of the pain to the same degree and intensity that you felt while actually going through the situation? Probably not. Of course you may remember the ordeal as being painful, but the point to understand here is that it no longer affects you in the same way — it does not hurt to the same degree.

Suffering from physical pain is similar to experiencing tragedy, hardship, or loss. The first days, months, and even years can seem unbearable. However, with time and a thankful outlook the pain will subside. What seems like intolerable pain at the time will eventually become a memory and the way you process experiences into memories can affect your outlook. Remember to view life in the big picture and to maintain trusting faith in God. When all is said and done, every experience you have will be a memory, leaving only your outlook. Make that outlook a positive, thankful one.

****

You can deal with whatever comes your way with a positive perspective. As long as you maintain thankfulness through your spiritual connection, tough, trying, or tragic times can no longer affect you in the same way.

****

4: Self-Pity

If you forget that adversity makes you stronger, it is all too easy to wallow in self-pity instead of giving thanks. You may have worrisome problems and troubles, but try not to think that your situation is the most challenging, tough, or grim circumstance that anyone has ever handled. By pitying yourself and your circumstances you are not being thankful for what you *do have.*

At times, life can certainly challenge us as we face difficult, seemingly overpowering situations. People may think they have grave problems, but the fact of the matter is that most of us do not. When we compare our problems to some of the real tragedies in our world, we soon realize that our troubles are simply a by-product of a selfish perspective.

I have come to know an older couple that provides a good example of feeling pity instead of thankfulness. They were healthy all of their lives, worked hard, and earned a good living that provided enough money to purchase a nice house, put food on the table, and still have some money in the bank. They set aside a sizable nestegg for the future. However, as sickness and general old age set in, they forgot the many, many blessings that had been bestowed upon them throughout their lives.

In the process of dealing with their present situation, they chose to see only the immediate problems and pain that confronted them, and forgot about the many good things they had been given. By forgetting their blessings of health, prosperity and a healthy, happy family, they failed to maintain a thankful view. They did not recognize the absolute bounty they had received throughout their lives and failed to completely understand that they were not entitled to any of it. This perspective caused them to become full of self-pity.

If this couple were to look back on their lives with an attitude of gratitude, they would feel blessed for being healthy the major part of their lives, as well as for their healthy family. Sure, the pain would still exist, and age would still take its toll; however, they would realize just how much they had received. A perspective of thankfulness would allow them to better cope with their current situation and empathize with the struggles other people go through, instead of becoming increasingly withdrawn, jealous, and embittered because of self-pity.

Thankful perspective: Try not to pity yourself because of your circumstances; be happy your situation is not worse. If you are going through a tough time, do not compare your pain and suffering to the blessings others may be receiving. Be thankful for your life, empathetic to the trials other people go through, and happy for others when good fortune embraces them.

Everyone will face tough times at some point in life, and feeling slighted or full of self-pity seems normal *only if* you do not have a thankful perspective. In fact, it is indeed easy for most people to pity themselves when they are selfishly preoccupied with what they think belongs to them. Self-pity is a negative characteristic that can be erased with a perspective of gratitude. Commit to learn techniques that will help change the negative patterns that self-pity produces.

5: Worry, Worry, Go Away...Relax!

Another major obstacle to being thankful is the human need to feel in control of life. People can be overcome with worry and speculation very easily when they don't realize just how much is out of the realm of our control. There are variables and situations that can be controlled, such as how hard you work, how much effort you put into life, and the choices you make. You may even have a sense of control, but that is a false perception. Although you can plan your future, set goals for yourself, and work diligently to achieve those goals, ultimately you are in control of very little.

How many times do people plan for a certain outcome and everything goes awry? Situations and circumstances are often beyond our control and we can fail to remember or recognize that fact when we get caught up with our own affairs. Concern and care (a.k.a. worry) does have a place and purpose, but excessive or misplaced worrying brings about negative thoughts and perspectives. This negativity spreads into all aspects of life and affects everything from your health to your interaction with others. For instance, I was involved with a wedding that was planned out meticulously. Every detail was planned, re-planned, and then thought about some more. The soon-to-be newlyweds were trying the patience and kindness of everyone who was helping them prepare for the big event, because they were getting a little obsessive about the whole production.

The young couple could not stand the thought of something going wrong with the wedding. By focusing narrowly on their particular wants and wishes, they became unnecessarily anxious and angry toward each other and toward their family and friends. They generated feelings of nervousness, stress, worry, and anger because they lost sight of what was truly in their control. Those feelings negatively affected everything about the situation.

Finally, after months and months of planning the big day arrived. After extracting every bit of energy and goodwill from themselves and those around them, the bride and groom were set. A few hours before the wedding was to start, the groom's father went on a last-minute errand. As the clock ticked closer to the wedding hour, he had not returned and everyone started to get understandably anxious. The time for the ceremony to start passed...fifteen minutes...forty minutes...an hour went by. Regrettably, the wedding party received the unwelcome news that the groom's father had suffered a massive heart attack and was in intensive care at a local hospital.

Thankful perspective: Try not to become so involved with trying to control your life that you forget what is really important.

Do not entertain the notion that adversity cannot find you. Losing sight of what you really control and becoming too involved with the details of life is a recipe for a rude awakening. Adversity finds everyone at some point and in some way — that is a fact over which you have no control. Granted, a wedding can be a most stressful time, and this particular wedding scenario may be an extreme example, but try to keep your sense of control in check regarding details and situations in life.

****

We can take steps to prepare for the situations that are within our control. We must plan and live for the future responsibly and carefully, but worrying about what is beyond our control causes unnecessary stress and obscures a thankful perspective.

****

We must be diligent and careful with life. That is a certainty. However, no one can stop a freak accident from happening or control other types of tragedy and loss. Learn to accept the fact that much of life is beyond our control.

****

Learn to let go of the uncontrollable aspects of life and pour that energy into being grateful for what you have received. Show gratefulness in thoughts, attitudes, and actions toward others. Most of us are blessed at one time or another. Remember those times and be thankful for them. When you feel worried — **STOP!** Try not to worry; give thanks every day for what you *do have*.

~ Maintain a Thankful Perspective ~

As you incorporate thankfulness into your life and remove the obstacles that hinder it, you can actively practice methods to help it take root and remain strong. Remember that your perception of life can allow you to find peace of mind and fulfillment regardless of what comes your way.

1: Your Thankful Checklist

The everyday things in life are so important that you must learn to be thankful for them as often as you can. I recognize that it is impossible to feel thankful 100 percent of the time, and everyone is guilty of taking things for granted sometimes, but establishing and reflecting on a "Things To Be Thankful For" checklist can help you strengthen your thankful perspective. Make a simple checklist of all that you are grateful for in life. Keep a copy close to your hand as well as your heart. Inventory the contents of your list frequently and constantly find more to add to it. Make it a habit to review your list daily.

First, be thankful for waking. Feel blessed to have another day — not just a day for you and your loved ones, but be grateful that the world has another sunrise. Now, if you can feel your limbs, give thanks. Can you hear? Can you see? Can you move at all? Can you think with a clear mind? If you answered yes to just one of these questions, be thankful. If you can say yes to more than one, then consider yourself truly blessed.

Be grateful every day for your health. If you are not healthy in some aspect, you can be thankful for the times you were healthy and for your current health in other areas. The same goes for your loved ones. Are your loved ones well now or have they had health at one time? Do not forget these times simply because they may be gone — give thanks for them

Review your list often and let thoughts of thankfulness permeate your mind. Over time, they will serve to strengthen your attitude of gratitude and work magic with your perspective. Continually add more items to your "Things To Be Thankful For" checklist and you will realize just how grateful you should be. Even when you are feeling down and life does not seem to be going your way, remember to review your checklist daily. Give thanks for all that is in your life by consciously recognizing what you have been given.

2: That's Life

Challenging circumstances and downright awful things can happen to anyone at any time. Life can be turned upside-down and changed forever in an instant. The difficulties of life fall upon everyone. One person may enjoy life at a particular moment while another may be suffering through tragedy. On the other hand, a person who may have suffered previously will enjoy blessings while someone else experiences hardship. Everyone goes through trials and tribulations and moments of negativity, but what determines success in dealing with adversity is the strength of your attitude of gratitude.

****

Thankfulness is a matter of perspective. With it you can find happiness and peace of mind no matter what challenges come your way. Without it you can become unhappy or despondent with life even if you have a great state of affairs.

****

Accept the fact that life may not turn out exactly as you dreamed. A key factor in remaining forever thankful is to accept that adversity will strike in some way. Do not be surprised when adversity comes to rest on you — it won't always happen to someone else. So many times I've heard people say, "I never thought this could happen to me."

Make every effort to remain consciously aware of the fact that something like "that" could happen to you at any time. Of course you shouldn't spend all of your time worrying about the many bad things that could happen. But be willing to accept the fact that you are not immune from difficulties of some kind and accept that you may come face to face with tough or tragic times. Be prepared to meet the challenges life throws your way with a thankful outlook.

All too often, we don't realize what we have until strong adversity is bearing down on us. If you are facing real tragedy, try to remember what your life was like before you were presented with serious problems. Do you look at others who are complaining about trivial or petty problems and tell yourself, "If I only had your problems?" When you are facing real troubles, it's not too late to appreciate the fact that you are given what you need in order to face and overcome them. If you haven't faced strong challenges yet, learn to view your petty problems and inconveniences as what they truly are by remembering that life could always be worse!

Life can seem rough and unfair, but as my grandmother always tells me, "The sun can't shine every day." There is much wisdom in that simple statement. Clouds and rain are just as important to our lives as the sun. Similarly, we need troubling times in life so that we can learn from them, grow from them, and appreciate our good times more because of them. Difficult times prove to be as necessary to life as the good times.

Life can be hard, but life happens. Cope with it while being thankful and fostering goodness. Do not be afraid of

lift his spirit and the spirits of those around him. The positive energy of his attitude worked wonders in all directions.

Unfortunately, as of this writing, Gary still fights the scourge of cancer, but he has no doubts about the future. He knows that many trials lie ahead of him, but his trusting faith and positive perspective of thankfulness remain unwavering. Ultimately, those things will help him and those around him to get through the tough and trying times ahead. I admire and respect his strength beyond words and I look to the example he sets through his actions and attitude as the thankfulness benchmark that each of us should aspire to reach.

We all know of situations that are incredibly trying. Millions of examples of tragedy exist. Along with those tragedies and the tough times that go with them are millions of examples of people maintaining thankful attitudes. Naturally, it isn't easy to feel thankful in extremely painful situations of tragedy and loss. However, follow the examples of gratitude that people set through adverse situations because it can be done. You can do it, too!

~ Give Thanks ~

Life is a learning process. We can choose to learn from every experience or we can wallow in pity and be thankless when life does not turn out as we plan. At times there is much pain in life, both perceived and real, but we must keep the faith. Always feel a sense of gratitude for the past and present, no matter what comes along.

As your attitude of gratitude becomes stronger, you will learn to accept that nothing in life is truly yours and that every part of life is just a loan, a lease that can be rescinded at any time. When you reach this point, you no longer feel like you can really lose anything even when you are faced with adversity and hardship.

A thankful perspective brings the knowledge and understanding that life is given to you. The fundamental awareness that life is ultimately in the control of SomeThing Greater than you becomes clear, and that brings peace of mind.

****

Feeling gratitude immediately or quickly is not always possible — do not become disheartened by that fact. Do your best to maintain a positive perspective.

****

Even though life can be painful, even unbearable at times, we have to remember that we will eventually understand if we have faith. When people ask why God allows bad things to happen, or why senseless violence occurs in our world every day, remember that we are not privy to understanding the biggest picture. We should give God the benefit of the doubt and give thanks for what we have been given.

A true perspective of thankfulness allows you to trust in God for all that happens in life. At the same time, your thankful attitude will give you strength and courage. You must care for your needs, plan for the future, and live your life, but an attitude of gratitude allows you to recognize that there is a bigger plan.

If your life is clouded with selfishness, you cannot maintain a thankful perspective. If you have been blessed with health, opportunities, and the ability to accomplish in life you must remember to *give* thanks. You can *give* thanks by becoming a person who shows gratitude by giving to others. Give money, time, or service. Remember, those things are not yours in the first place — they were gifts to you first. Do not be greedy with what you have and give while you are able. Life can change in an instant and your gifts and the ability to give can be taken from you. Learn to become a selfless, giving person. Give thanks.

✓ To Do List: Look Up — Be Thankful

❑ **Look up — be thankful.**

❑ **Thank God:**
—The foundation of a thankful perspective starts by giving thanks to God.

❑ **Be thankful for each new day:**
—Every day is a gift — for you personally, as well as for the world.

❑ **Be thankful for your health:**
—Remember that your health is ultimately not in your hands.
—Recognize that health covers many different aspects.
—Be thankful for the health with which you're blessed.

❑ **Be thankful for your abilities:**
—Realize that your abilities are a gift.
—Be humble as you remember that your accomplishments are not completely yours.

❑ **Remove obstacles that hinder a thankful perspective.**

❑ **Stop taking things for granted:**
—Consciously think about and be grateful for what is in your life every day.
—Show gratitude in thought as well as action.

❑ **Do not feel entitled to the things you receive from God.**

—Recognize that you are not entitled to health, happiness, or a good life from God—they are gifts you receive.

—Be thankful for, and humbled by, the gifts you receive.

❑ **Be willing to accept that adversity may strike at any time in life.**

❑ **Be thankful through tough times.**

—Always find something to be thankful for, no matter what situation you are going through.

—Find thankful ways to deal with tough situations.

❑ **Do not pity yourself because of circumstances in life:**

—View life with thankfulness instead of pity.

—Do not compare your problems with the problems of others.

—Be thankful, because your situation could always be worse.

—View adversity as something that will make you stronger.

—Be happy for others when good fortune embraces them.

❑ **Try not to worry about what cannot be controlled:**

—Learn what is yours to control because much of life is beyond your control.

71

—Do not get so caught up with the details of life that you forget to act with thankfulness and goodness.

—Convert the energy spent on worrying into thankful thoughts and actions.

❑ **Strengthen your thankful perspective.**

❑ **Create your "Things To Be Thankful For:" checklist:**

—Reflect on and write down everything you should be thankful for, from a new day, to health, to the goodness of humanity.

—Review your checklist several times a day and add to it often.

❑ **Maintain an attitude of gratitude to the best of your ability:**

—Take heart in the fact that people have gone through terrible situations and have been able to maintain a thankful perspective. So can you!

—Share some of the gifts you receive with others.

—Remember that a life clouded with selfishness cannot maintain a thankful perspective.

❑ **A thankful perspective must be coupled with thankful actions of goodness.**

Notes:

CHAPTER 6

Look Within to Change
Find selflessness within.

"We must look within ourselves
to find that which we seek in others."
—Ken William

Having faith, connecting to goodness, and maintaining a thankful perspective begin the process of getting back to good. Becoming selfless is the next essential step in completing that process. Both selfishness and selflessness are part of human nature. While selfishness is necessary for survival, it can be taken beyond that original, positive intent. Selflessness is also necessary for survival, although for different reasons. We have the ability to control our instincts, but we can have trouble maintaining balance between them. We often act more selfishly than we should and just as often, we don't follow our selfless instincts to their full potential. To understand why, we must look within.

Excessive selfishness is an aspect of human nature that is responsible for many of humanity's problems. It brings a host of negative emotions and actions into individual lives as well as into our world. These range from having petty arguments or difficulties with those around us, to phenomenal amounts of greed, jealousy, violence, and self-centeredness. Excessive selfishness is not a condition that afflicts just one country, society, or belief. It is a universal, undesirable trait found throughout the human family. Luckily, it is a trait that can be changed.

Why are human beings selfish? Why are we selfless? Though many of us are taught to be selfless by parents, mentors, and religious and spiritual teachings, we often think and behave more selfishly than we should. Acting selfishly is a *choice* that brings intolerance, greed, and jealousy into our lives. At the same time, we can choose to be selfless by giving to others and fostering kindness, tolerance, and goodness. Selfless actions prove that it is possible for people to look beyond individual needs in order to give.

While instincts drive us to act both selflessly and selfishly, we ultimately have the freedom to choose between them. The notion of people acting selfishly is quite easy to justify and understand — we have to care for our needs and well-being in order to survive. However, understanding why we should be selfless may not be quite so obvious. Selfless actions are as important as caring for our material wants and needs. Perhaps they are even more important. Remember, we have the ability to choose to be the working definition of positive or negative, to live with selflessness or to be excessively selfish. Ultimately, we are responsible for our thoughts and actions and we must choose wisely.

~ Why are Human Beings Selfish? ~

All living things use selfishness as a mechanism for self-preservation. In the natural scheme of life, individuals of every species are bound by the innate knowledge of what must be done to survive physically (selfish behaviors). The priority for living beings is to protect and nurture what is important to survival of the individual and of the species.

Survival of the fittest is a law of nature stating that the strong will survive. The strong are able to harness what they need for survival through their attributes, talents, and physical abilities, thereby prospering while the weak and less fortunate become a part of history. Nature, outside of humanity, runs perfectly with this design in place because life takes only what it needs to survive. There are no drives or desires other than those for basic survival, with no waste, no want, and no excess.

The self-preservation (selfish) programming that works so well in nature becomes radically changed when applied to human intellect, traits, and emotions. Human beings think and act with selfishness because those feelings and tendencies are instinctively wired into the psyche to allow for physical self-preservation. Problems occur because we can easily incorporate selfishness into areas of life where it does not belong.

~ Why are Human Beings Selfless? ~

Survival instincts for human beings are similar to those of other forms of life in many respects, yet vastly different overall. Of course, we have to maintain life-sustaining behaviors in order to stay alive, but self-preservation for human beings goes beyond mere physical survival. Our instinctual needs also require us to seek spirituality, purpose, and meaning for life. These needs are fulfilled in large part through our selfless instincts.

Why are people selfless toward others when it is not necessary for physical survival? The answer to that question lies in the fact that selflessness is programmed into the human brain to fulfill the more complex areas of self-preservation — soul or spirit preservation, if you will. When you give to someone or promote goodness in some way, you are doing something that directly benefits you. Some people may question the validity of that statement but in the end, you will find truth. (You will come to know when you understand.)

~ **Our Dilemma** ~

Each of us faces a dilemma as we try to maintain a proper balance between our selfish and selfless instincts. How do we balance these driving forces? To a certain extent our intellect allows us to control instincts with reason, logic, and emotion, although there are times when a person can act or react purely on instinct. The task of controlling or balancing our instincts is helped by the fact that every human being has the innate ability to fundamentally know right from wrong. We call this ability conscience.

****

The issue of "right and wrong" is highly subjective, but the concept I am referring to here is inherent in the human mind. Generally speaking, when you do harm to or forcibly take something from someone or something else, we consider your actions wrong. Of course, many degrees of right and wrong apply to many different situations. Please interpret it here at a most fundamental level.

****

Conflicts arising between our instincts and our intellect cause a dilemma for us. Because we are free to choose our own thoughts and actions, we have the power to interpret and control our instincts. The problem is that selfishness can dominate our selfless intuition quite easily and cause us to think and act more selfishly than we should.

Debates rage concerning whether humans are born with selfish and selfless instincts or whether those traits are learned as people grow. In my opinion, both nature and nurture play a role in our thoughts and actions. Selfishness is ingrained in the human mind as an instinct, and so is selflessness. Either may seem more or less prevalent in any one person, but they are both programmed in the brain.

Verification of the instinctual programming in the human mind is evident in many ways. One such verification is the fact that you feel satisfied when you complete a task related to instinct. When you are hungry and fulfill that hunger by eating, you feel a sense of satisfaction. When you are thirsty, and then drink, you feel good — satisfied. Caring for your needs brings instinctual satisfaction. Accordingly, we can see that selflessness is also programmed into the mind because when you carry out selfless actions, you feel good. Giving to someone or offering some type of assistance brings a sense of fulfillment. That inherent satisfaction comes from fulfilling your selfless instincts.

Another method of determining human instincts is to look at the actions of very young children (approximately 1–2 years old) because they are predominantly instinctual. Nowhere is human nature more pure or easier to view than in the behaviors of a young child. The part of the brain that can control or modify instinctual behaviors is not yet completely developed, so actions reflect the pure, instinctual programming of the mind. The following examples are admittedly elementary and the scope of this book does not support scientific documentation, but they effectively demonstrate basic instinctual behaviors.

The fact that young children act selfishly is not a new discovery. In fact, they show selfishness in a number of different ways. For instance, if a child wants something and cannot get it, he may cry or throw tantrums until the matter is forgotten or until the desire is satisfied. Another example of selfish behavior occurs when a child has something she is not willing to share. How many parents remember that their child's first words were "No!" or "Mine!"? If the child has not yet developed speech, she may rely on a piercing scream or a slight demonstration of physical force to communicate the desire to keep what she wants. Is the child consciously thinking about acting in such ways? Has the child been taught to be selfish at this tender age? Of course not. The child simply knows that he wants, and the thoughts and actions of pure, selfish instincts are revealed.

Thankfully, children also show actions that are selfless in nature. They may show signs of selfless giving, such as sharing a toy, offering some of their lunch, or showing compassion to someone who is hurt. Again, they do not act in these ways because they are taught to or are consciously thinking about doing so. They inherently know how to act selflessly. These actions are pure — the instinctual programming of the human mind translated directly into action.

As children grow, instinctual behaviors are molded by the experiences, rules, instructions, and guidance received from those around them. The upbringing and environment in which a child grows up exerts major influences on perceptions and perspectives that meld with unique traits to form a distinctive personality. These factors work collectively with intellect and emotion to affect the choices and decisions that each of us make throughout life.

~ We *Choose* our Choices ~

People make choices. Every day we are faced with the task of making decisions. Those decisions can move us toward goodness or cause us to stray from it. Either way, the ability to choose our choices remains our own. People may act in ways that are completely opposite to their upbringing. For instance, if a person has been raised in a selfless home full of goodness, he or she may choose to act selfishly. In contrast, a child who faces a preponderance of selfishness can still grow to become a positive, selfless, successful person. These outcomes may be a result of external influences, innate behaviors, or a combination of several factors, but they are ultimately the result of choice.

Selfless instincts must be nurtured and reinforced during formative years in order for them to take root and become a driving force later in life. A person's childhood can be filled with so much negativity that connecting with selfless instincts becomes virtually impossible. Consequently, we must constantly stress the importance of caring for children with love and goodness. However, while childhood environment plays a major role in the way a person thinks and acts as an adult, it is ultimately up to each person to direct his or her energies toward selfless thoughts and actions. Instincts, personality, and upbringing can only affect us to a certain degree. We ultimately control our thoughts and actions.

Our common urge to blame someone or something else for our selfish behavior may seem justified at times, but it is almost always wrong. Thoughts and actions are the responsibility of each individual. Each of us inherently knows what is fundamentally right or wrong and we can choose how to think and act. No one can force a person to live with goodness because every human being is accountable for his or her selfless actions (or lack thereof).

~ Selfishness is Abundant ~

Although countless thoughts and actions of selflessness occur every day, their effects are diminished by the numerous selfish actions that are more abundant than we realize. Violent, vicious, and evil actions often capture the spotlight; but selfishness is not limited to actions that are destructive, wicked, or large in scope. The smaller actions of selfishness, ranging from personal intolerance, impoliteness, and greed, to selfish spirituality or thinking in "me" terms, all detract from goodness in the same way.

****

Selfish behaviors, large and small, must be identified and changed in order to get back to good.
****

Selfishness is abundant because we incorporate it into areas of life where it does not belong. This causes us to focus too intensely on ourselves, blurring the line between our wants and our needs. The selfish mind thinks in "me" terms, spawning negative emotions and traits, such as jealousy, greed, and false pride.

For the selfish person, everything is "all about me." They believe statements like the following: "My way of doing things is the only right way; my religion is the only right one; my family is the most important; my problems are the worst; my life matters most." This type of thinking hinders goodness by causing pain, separation, ill will, and suffering, clearly leading to more negativity in general.

~ Selfish to Selfless ~

Every person has the ability to think and act with selflessness, and each of us can find more ways to do so. Recall your selfless instincts with conscious effort and allow them to come through in thought and action. By practicing selfless beliefs and behaviors, you can restore balance to your instincts. You have the choice to control your actions in a selfless way — the choice is *yours*. Obviously, some people will choose not to act selflessly toward you; however, you cannot use that as an excuse to act selfishly.

Since you have lived through a unique set of circumstances and experiences, your personal self-preservation is something you must figure out for yourself. Look at your life thoroughly and think about what you have, and what you have to give. Are you as selfless as you can be? Are you able to objectively view yourself and find room for improvement? How elaborate do your material possessions need to be? Do you look down on others? Are you intolerant or envious of others? Think about these questions and add more of your own. Be willing to accept the fact that you may have some work to do in order to become more selfless.

Like any living thing, human beings must focus on themselves in order to survive. But unlike other creatures, we have the ability to differentiate between what we want and what we need. Often, we know what we need but we still *want* excessively beyond that point. We are all guilty of this to one extent or another, and have to learn to realize when we have an adequate amount in our lives. Your thoughts and actions are personal choices, so no one can make them, correct them, or account for them except you. Your responsibility is to bring goodness into the world by changing selfish thoughts, emotions, and actions into selfless ones.

✓ To Do List: Look Within to Change

❑ **Understand why selfishness exists:**
—Selfishness is wired into the mind for physical survival.

❑ **Understand why selflessness exists:**
—Selflessness is wired into the mind for higher levels of self-preservation that are as important as the physical aspects of survival, if not more so.

❑ **Work to control your selfishness.**

❑ **Empower yourself to live with goodness by encouraging your selfless instincts.**

❑ **Identify selfish thoughts and behaviors, large and small:**
—Do not rationalize that you are not selfish simply because you have not broken any laws or committed significant actions of selfishness.
—Recognize that selfishness covers everything from physically hurting someone, to intolerance, to stealing, to making fun of someone.

❑ **Selfishness can be changed:**
—You are responsible for fostering goodness by replacing selfishness with selflessness.

❑ **Make a personal to-do list to encourage selflessness:**

Notes:

Chapter 7

Selfish to Selfless

Identify your selfishness and learn to become selfless.

"Only a life lived for others is worth living."
—Albert Einstein

Why does it seem like such a struggle for people to be selfless? Even though we inherently know that being selfless is a moral, virtuous thing, many people fail to act selflessly to their full potential. The reasons for this shortcoming are many: we can choose to be selfish; we may have forgotten how to be selfless; or maybe haven't even considered being selfless.

Do you think you are selfish? Do you *know* you are? Do you honestly admit, "It's all about me," and believe that's okay? For many people, any type of giving, sharing, or patience beyond personal needs can seem to be a challenge at times (myself included). Everyone fits somewhere between the extremes of being purely selfless and purely selfish. There is room for improvement no matter where you fit.

Learn to identify and overcome selfishness in order to get back to good. However, remember that the road from selfishness to selflessness can be bumpy and difficult to travel. You may make some wrong turns along the way and get lost from time to time, but you can always find your way back. You will travel this road every day of your life because selflessness requires daily effort and maintenance. Treating others with selflessness — as you deserve to be treated — is not a new idea, but one that is often ignored. Look beyond self-service and strive to become more selfless.

To start, reflect on how we neglect to treat one another as we should. People are not as kind or courteous to others as they could be. Many are quick to anger, usually for petty, trivial reasons. The slight inconveniences that inevitably occur can be blown out of proportion and handled in a selfish manner. Everyone is so busily involved with *their* lives, *their* troubles, and *their* wants, that it becomes increasingly difficult to accommodate even the smallest actions of selflessness.

Without small actions of selflessness, hope inevitably wanes for selfless thoughts and actions on a grander scale. When hope is gone, we practically invite excessive selfishness into our lives, and all of us fall into a downward spiral of negativity. This includes our leaders, organizations, and even entire countries. Changing that downward spiral is such an enormous task that we can rationalize and justify being selfish by believing that we are helpless to affect change on our own. After all, what can one person do to stem the tide of selfishness in our world?

The truth is far more hopeful, however. When people replace selfishness with selflessness, the tiny seeds of goodness are planted and begin to grow. Sometimes goodness grows subtly, but it also grows exponentially. A little selflessness goes a long way toward bringing our world back to good, and each of us has room to expand our selfless horizons.

In order to become selfless, we must acknowledge and be fully aware of our selfish tendencies. The following definitions and categories will help assess where your thoughts and actions fit on a selfish/selfless scale. This assessment will enable you to see what you need to do in order to bring more selflessness into your life.

****

The following general definitions are by no means all-inclusive. Please add your own insights to them.

****

~ Defining Selflessness ~

Selflessness, by definition, is the nature of people who are truly generous individuals. Selfless instincts are always at the forefront of their minds, demonstrated by the fact that they put the needs of others first. They will give to anyone, at any time, often surrendering or sacrificing something of their own in the process. They realize that nothing in life is truly their own, and they offer help, kindness, and material assistance to the best of their ability.

Selfless people give because they inherently comprehend that giving is the right thing to do. The willingness to give comes as naturally as breathing to them. They do not give to receive attention or because they expect something in return. Their selfless acts of giving are small and large, ranging from being courteous while driving to giving donations; from volunteering time to taking the first steps in order to repair a broken relationship. In addition, they give as freely to those they do not know as they do to their loved ones.

Another trait of truly selfless people is tolerance. This tolerance extends over every aspect of their lives. They will not judge based on appearance, spiritual beliefs, race, or preconceived ideas or stereotypes, and they offer respect to everyone. They will not look down on another person regardless of social, economic, or educational class. Selfless people know and remember the fact that everyone is equal, and they do not feel that their personal way of doing things is exclusively correct.

Genuinely selfless people are forgiving and readily offer apologies. They do not hold grudges, and are able to put aside personal pride if it means helping someone or mending a broken relationship.

Finally, selfless people are genuinely nice, approachable, warm, and friendly. They offer patience in situations where most people would become angry. Rather than becoming impatient, they offer encouragement to help rectify a situation. Kindness is always a companion to their giving, and the recipients of their selflessness never feel as if something is owed.

~ Defining Selfishness ~

Selfish people are those who primarily care about themselves to the exclusion of others, but the definition goes far beyond that. The concept of selfishness encompasses all selfish thoughts and behaviors, up to and including purely evil actions. Luckily, the vast majority of people suffer from a perspective that is far less severe. Selfish people live in a clouded bubble, dealing exclusively with what pertains directly to them. Blindly going about their lives by thinking only of what benefits them, they are not able to see that being selfless is necessary and good. Rarely will they look outside their bubble of selfishness and even when they do, their perceptions are as blurry and distorted as if they were looking through a real bubble.

Selfish people cannot comprehend why a person would give to someone without being forced to do so. They believe in the necessity of gaining something in return for any act of giving. In other words, they would only give in order to receive some benefit in return. Their perspective causes them to tend exclusively to what affects *them,* inside of *their* bubble. Unfortunately, they never pop the bubble or find a way to give to others outside of it because their perspective does not allow them to recognize the joy of helping and giving to others.

As selfish people sit in their self-inflicted confines, their distorted view of reality affects every aspect of their lives. Self-centeredness causes them to become too close to their lives, material belongings, and problems (which are usually mere inconveniences). This begins the "it's all about me" complex. Even if life is going their way, they always find something to complain about. If life happens to place some bumps in the road, their complaints turn into tantrums. As selfishly minded people gain more material possessions, success, perceived power, or status, they always want more. They are never satisfied or thankful for what they do have.

At some point, the selfishness of these people affects the lives of those around them. They may look at others who have received a blessing, be it in family, money, or success, and go so far as to begrudge the recipient of that blessing. The selfish mind tends to think, "No one should have anything if I don't. I should not be made to suffer, struggle, or do without unless everyone else shares the same fate." They cannot enjoy someone else's happiness and good fortune because they always want more for themselves. Instead of taking a thankful perspective, selfish people are trapped in a circle of negativity where they constantly worry about what others may be getting or have received. They feel shorted, cheated, and slighted by life, society, and even God.

Selfish people are intolerant. Their actions range from ignorance and impoliteness to prejudice, spite, or hatred based on racial, social, educational, or spiritual differences. They feel superior to others for superficial and egotistical reasons and often feel as if they have to tolerate other human beings. When they have to deal with others, they may act aggressively or be condescending. Selfish minds believe that other people are beneath them. (The selfish mind can have much brain but very little mind. Translation: a selfish person can be well versed and successful in the practical areas of life, but may lack and ignore the knowledge of how to treat others with goodness.) Of course, the selfish mind cannot or will not see its own faults or mistakes because for this type of mindset, it truly is "all about me."

Remember, you do not have to commit terrible acts of selfishness or do great harm to others to be considered a selfish individual. Caring only for your own needs can mark you as a selfish person. If you do not care for others, you are nurturing selfishness and moving away from goodness.

~ Selfless/Selfish Levels ~

Now that you have general definitions of selflessness and selfishness, you can begin organizing those definitions into a scale with different categories as you assess your own placement. Levels of selflessness and selfishness can be separated into five general categories, each open to your personal interpretation. Each level contains elements of the definitions of selflessness or selfishness, and some levels incorporate elements of both definitions. The levels are as follows:

1. Completely Selfless = Goodness
2. Generally Selfless = Givers
3. Selfishly Selfless = Givers and Takers
4. Selfish = Takers
5. Excessive / Evil Selfishness = Evil Takers

At one end of the scale lies the ideal goodness of complete selflessness. At the other end is the extreme of excessive, evil selfishness. Everyone thinks and acts in ways that put them at some point between complete selflessness and excessive selfishness. Place yourself into the level or levels that best describes you.

****

Your placement in these categories is for you to decide. You may need an objective opinion from people who know you in order to make an accurate placement. Consult those who know you well; ask them to offer opinions and candid observations in order to help you assess your proper category. This, in turn, can bring you closer to selflessness — closer to goodness.

****

The following chart shows a rough distribution of the relative percentage of the human population that falls into each category.

Selfless and selfish levels (Percent of population)*

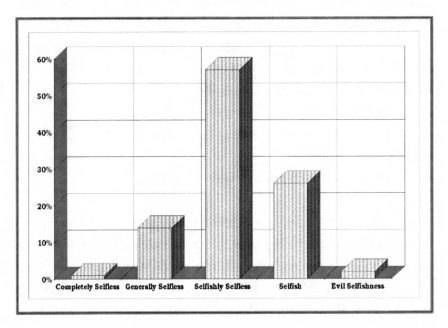

*Author's Subjective Percentages

Read the following descriptions to find which one best describes where you fit. Remember to incorporate the general definitions of selflessness and selfishness and add your own insights to those definitions. Once you have a point of reference, you can begin to work toward becoming more selfless.

#1: Completely Selfless

—An idealistic definition of selflessness — GOODNESS.

Complete selflessness is more of an ideal, rather than an attainable level of human ability. However, an extremely small percentage of humanity manages to truly fit into this category by consistently sustaining a lifestyle that entails giving to others in thought, action, and attitude. They live for others, understanding and showing the true meaning of life: to give, to be helpful, to show tolerance and care, to offer forgiveness, and to live with goodness. Their thoughts and deeds are selflessly directed toward others, as well as toward the very nature that supports life. Selfish actions, beyond the basic needs of survival, are non-existent in their lives.

#2: Generally Selfless

—Thinking and acting as the working definition of selflessness, yet on occasion, acting in a slightly selfish manner — GIVERS.

This level describes people who exemplify the traits that define selflessness. They consistently offer themselves to others in any capacity possible. The vast majority of their thoughts and actions are selfless, with only minor, infrequent actions of selfishness. Emotions, feelings, and circumstances in life can cause a generally selfless person to lose their way from true selflessness from time to time, although very rarely. A person in this category would never intentionally hurt, harm, or cause pain to someone else because of selfishness. More than likely, people who truly belong in this category would not place themselves in it, as they always feel they could be more selfless.

#3: Selfishly Selfless

—Thinking and acting in a manner that incorporates the definitions of selflessness and selfishness to varying degrees — GIVERS and TAKERS.

The vast majority of humanity belongs in this level. Selfishly selfless people maintain characteristics and actions that fit into the descriptions of both selflessness and selfishness to varying degrees. People who fit in this level care for themselves and the needs and wants of others, but they do not carry out acts of selflessness to their full potential. They are well-meaning, good-natured people who simply do not live as selflessly as they could. At times, selfless thoughts and actions may only apply to those who are important to them, such as family and friends, while they show something less than selflessness toward others (or vice versa).

Selfishly selfless people can be judgmental and hurtful. Examples range from getting upset over the everyday situations of life to holding grudges; from maintaining a view of superior or exclusively righteous beliefs to showing slight amounts of prejudice toward those who are different. They may believe that any perspective that differs from theirs is incorrect. Such a view invariably results in some degree of intolerance and judgment, but this person will never tolerate the extremes of hatred or violence. Selfishly selfless individuals act selflessly by giving to others, offering help, kindness, and forgiveness, and by showing genuine concern and compassion, but to a lesser degree than is possible. Remember, the majority of humanity fits somewhere into this level, with ample room for improvement.

#4: Selfish

—Thinking and acting according to the definition of selfishness, up to, but not including violent or evil thoughts and actions — TAKERS

This category covers people who care exclusively for themselves. They often lead socially correct lives, function well in society, and become materially successful by caring for what is important to them. However, everything in life is "all about them." They only look for ways to benefit themselves, protect what is "theirs" to an unreasonable degree, and do not care for the needs, feelings, or wishes of a person who is outside their perspective or wants. A selfish person does not consider giving to others for the sake of goodness.

People in this level are intolerant and judgmental. If your beliefs are not like their beliefs, then you are wrong. If you are not in the same social, racial, or educational class, they will look down on you, be intolerant of you, or try to degrade you for your differences. Selfish people maintain perspectives of superiority and believe that they are better than others. They choose not to acknowledge the fact that people are fundamentally equal.

#5: Evil/Extreme Selfishness

—Thinking and acting in a completely selfish manner. Becoming the definition of selfishness through violent and evil actions to satisfy selfish desires — EVIL TAKERS.

Those who care exclusively for themselves and break laws of humanity, society, and goodness in order to get what they desire fall into this category. They will use force, violence, deceit, or any other evil, heinous, or atrocious action in order to satisfy their wants. Their mindset allows them to justify their thoughts and actions.

People who fit in this level do not think about how their actions will affect others. They lack and/or ignore any sense of right and wrong, do not have remorse about any evil or harm they have committed, and are not affected by conscience. True spirituality is non-existent in their lives. Any perceived spirituality or connection to God is grossly disfigured from true goodness (i.e. to kill in the name of a particular belief or inflict harm on others because they are not of the same spiritual faith, race, nation, or social class).

Only a relatively small percentage of humanity fits into this category. That fact may be hard to accept because of the preponderance of negativity reported in the media, but out of the six billion people that inhabit our world, only a minuscule number actually fall into this category. Unfortunately, evil actions, and the people who commit them, get inordinate amounts of attention.

~ **Where Do You Fit?** ~

Determine where you fit within the levels. You may fit into more than one category due to the many different situations and dynamic circumstances you come across in life. Remember, you may have a more selfish perspective than you realize, so your assessment may not be entirely accurate. Ask people who know you well to objectively and candidly describe you in order to help point out some of your traits and tendencies. Do not get angry or defensive about their view, but consider their comments as tools for you to make a proper assessment that can ultimately help you become more selfless.

****

Honestly rate yourself. You may need to get some insight into your tendencies and behaviors from people who can give you an objective assessment. Unless you are willing to accept that you are selfish in some aspects of life, change will not be possible.

****

If you feel that you are not selfish, you should reassess your thoughts and actions, past and present, and take a closer look. Maybe you are not as tolerant as you should be. For instance, does race or physical appearance play a role in how you view a person? Are you tolerant of other spiritual or religious beliefs, or do you think your views are exclusively correct? There are other avenues available to explore. Do you gossip or silently wish ill or harm to others? Are you jealous of the possessions, lifestyle, or accomplishments of others? Are you selfless only with your loved ones, but not toward other people (or vice versa)? Do you outwardly show selflessness, but think the opposite? Are you easily upset in situations that require patience? Are you judgmental? Do apologies, forgiveness, and thankfulness flow easily from your mind as well as your mouth? Take a close, objective look at your thoughts and actions and find areas where you need improvement.

~ Become Selfless ~

How did your personal assessment go? After identifying your problem areas, make a list of your selfish thoughts and actions — don't forget the small things. Draft a plan to correct selfish tendencies by writing down what you can do in order to change and then put that plan into action. Remember, moving to selflessness is a process that takes effort and time. Start small and be consistent in your approach.

Selfishness turns into selflessness in a number of ways. Simple daily actions, such as smiling and saying hello to someone walking by or being genuinely nice to others are a great start. You can hold a door for someone, be patient while driving, offer an apology, and make the first call to repair a relationship. Say thank you. Hold your temper. Give of yourself in any number of different ways to people you know, as well as to those you don't know. Giving selflessly can be accomplished by sharing kindness, forgiveness, tolerance, patience, time, encouragement, compassion, and material help, to name just a few.

Many people consider themselves to be selfless, but they can be quick to balk or stop short when an opportunity to be kind or giving to others is presented to them. They can have difficulty extending even the smallest actions of selflessness, such as leaving a generous tip at a restaurant, saying thank you, offering to pay for something, giving tolerance, or showing kindness and patience in everyday actions. They can be self-centered regarding faith and they seem to forget that true spirituality demands goodness, selflessness, *and* tolerance.

Do not let this become the case for you. Be less concerned with telling others how selfless you are and let your actions be your voice. Small measures of selflessness are just as important as grand ones because they build the foundation for becoming a more giving, selfless person. All of your thoughts and actions can be infused with selfless giving, and *every* such action brings you closer to goodness.

When you wander from the path of goodness (and we all will), your selfless acts can lose value. For instance, if someone gives to you in some way, yet treats you badly in other ways, their selfless acts can lose value. Therefore, it is especially important to be as consistent as possible with selfless behaviors. Of course, there will be times when you fall short and make mistakes — being selfless is not always easy. If you wander from the path, be sure to find your way back to it.

~ Judge Your Own Selfishness ~

Many people self-righteously label those who are well off in some area of life as being selfish. Who is able to draw the distinction between what is too much and just enough as it pertains to lifestyle or possessions? For example, a person who earns an average wage and owns a modest house may believe that a well-off person with a substantial home has "too much". To that person, "too much" may mean someone who owns several lavish houses on three continents, a 300-foot yacht, and other materialistic luxuries. However, to a person struggling to put food on the table and pay the rent, the person with a modest house may seem to have "too much." Finally, a person who has given up most of his worldly possessions to selflessly help others may view everyone who does not give to that same degree as having "too much." This begs the question: Who can definitively judge what is considered too much?

How much does one person need? Only that one person can answer this question. No one has the right to say what is too much or incorrect regarding the material possessions or lifestyles of others, as long as no hurt or harm is caused. You may express what would be correct for yourself, but you should not judge other people — that is not an action of goodness.

Material possessions and lifestyle, as long as they cause no hate, harm, or intolerance, are a matter of perspective and personal choice. (That's not to say that those choices are spiritually or morally correct. I am merely pointing out that you and I do not have the right to judge.) Every person is responsible for deciding his or her individual actions and every individual is ultimately held accountable for those actions. Again, do not judge others based on their choices as long as they cause no hate, harm, or intolerance. Rather, apply judgment to yourself and choose to find more goodness in your own life.

Do not automatically stereotype an individual as selfish simply because of financial means. Wealth, in and of itself, is not necessarily an indicator of selfishness. Only actions toward others are. A person who is well off financially can be as kind, generous, and giving as a person who has means that are more modest. Indeed, people of modest means can be as stingy, self-centered, and selfish as the night is dark. Learn to look at a person's attitude of selflessness instead of looking at what he or she owns. Remember, the person decides how to act, not his or her possessions.

****

Having a selfless attitude toward others is far more important than wealth or material possessions. The simple action of not judging others is an action of selflessness that brings you closer to goodness.

****

Concern yourself with your choices, instead of judging the actions and possessions of others. Ultimately, you must justify and account for *your* thoughts, actions, and lifestyle — no one else's. Act with selflessness and tolerance, instead of passing judgment.

~ Be Selfless ~

Being selfless will help you find purpose in life. Sustaining and caring for your needs and the needs of your loved ones are lofty and admirable goals. However, if that is all you strive for, you may not be fulfilling a part of your destiny. (I know that sounds dramatic, but it just might have some truth to it.) Take a step back from the life you are given and realize that you are sometimes selfish. It may be difficult for you to recognize your selfish thoughts and behaviors, but do not let this discourage you. Let it motivate you to learn how to recognize and shun selfishness.

Any selfless act, whether giving something you own, offering a nice gesture, or being tolerant, will expand and grow exponentially as it touches the lives of others. A single act of selflessness that is done for the sake of goodness will give rise to more thoughts and actions of goodness. Everyone you come in contact with can be inspired in such a beneficial way that the overall positive effects are nearly impossible to imagine. Selflessness is most effective and matters most when it is consistently applied to all areas of life, even to your everyday actions. Become selfless to the best of your ability.

✓ To Do List: Selfish to Selfless

❑ **Assess your thoughts and actions of selfishness.**

❑ **Rate yourself on the selfish/selfless scale:**
—Get an objective opinion to help you identify what you need to work on.
—List your selfish behaviors, make a plan, and commit to change your selfish thoughts and actions.

❑ **Be selfless to the best of your ability.**

❑ **Do not judge others with respect to their possessions or lifestyle, as long as no hurt or harm is caused:**
—Recognize that everyone is accountable for his or her own lifestyle and actions.

❑ **Ways that I am selfish:**
➤ _____
➤ _____

❑ **What I need to do in order to be more selfless:**
➤ _____
➤ _____

Notes:

CHAPTER 8

Get Back to Good By Giving

Give selflessly.

*"You make a living by what you get,
but you make a life by what you give."*
—Winston Churchill

It's normal and healthy for us to be interested in the things that directly affect us, but we are meant to do much more. We cannot be involved in everything that occurs in our family, community, or world; however, most of us are able to direct a much larger part of our lives toward giving in some way.

A major component of getting back to good is to give selflessly to others. Your thoughts and actions are the only things you truly own so they are essentially the only things that you can give to others. As the keeper of your kindness, your tolerance, your positive attitude of gratitude, and your patience, you have the responsibility to give those things. Share them often and give freely.

The act of giving is a way of putting selfless thoughts and aspirations directly into action. To give, in the truest sense of the word, means to do so for the sake of giving goodness. You do not give because you expect to get something in return, but because you know in your heart that it is the right thing to do. Find a way to give.

Selfless giving can be accomplished in many ways at many different levels. It incorporates helping others, caring for nature and the environment, and offering tolerance and forgiveness. Selfless giving includes gifts of your patience, kindness, compassion, and empathy, as well as time, money, encouragement, and a positive attitude.

The extent to which you give makes little difference on the scales of goodness. The important thing is for you *to give*. For instance, if you are only able to donate a small amount of money or time, do not fret — give what you can at this moment. Give what you can when you can. Remember, giving your patience in a traffic jam is akin to making a monetary donation. Different ways of giving merely reflect unique aspects of selflessness.

All ways of giving are connected, and each one matters. One particular method of giving is no better than any other — at heart, they are one and the same. When you give kindness, you are giving help. When you are tolerant, you are being kind. When you are patient and polite, you give help, kindness, and tolerance. The act of giving is what is important, ultimately transforming into goodness.

~ Give Tolerance ~

Diversity is a law of nature, and the diversity of humanity is natural and worthy of tolerance. Human beings feel comfortable with things that are familiar to them. That being said, we should be very tolerant of one another despite our superficial differences, because we are essentially the same. Genetically, we are cut from the same cloth. Our meager genetic differences are what give us outward differences in skin color, height, and other physical characteristics. Add to these our cultural, spiritual, and personal differences and we still have no justification for intolerance. No human being has the right to dictate what should be tolerated regarding different beliefs, characteristics, lifestyles, or perspectives, as long as those things do not promote hatred or harm.

Simply because a person is different from you in some way does not give you the right or justification to be intolerant of that diversity. By the same token, you must not feel superior or better than someone else because of differences. There are many ways to live that differ from the ways you may choose and they are each as valid as yours. The beauty of our world stems from the very diversity all around us.

****

An important way to foster goodness in life is to be tolerant of others. Intolerance encompasses everything from disliking someone because of looks, such as race, dress, or physical appearance, to being intolerant of a person's beliefs, lifestyle, or personality.

****

Intolerance does not have to be outwardly expressed to be hurtful. When you harbor intolerant thoughts, you are fooling and hurting yourself because those thoughts will affect your outlook. Eventually your intolerance may be expressed in your words or actions even if you are not consciously aware of it. When you are intolerant of others for any reason, you are also being intolerant of yourself.

~ Personal Tolerance ~

Every individual has distinctive viewpoints and opinions. These differences result from your unique beliefs, personality, and life experiences. Your views, perspectives, and opinions are correct and true for you. They are not necessarily the best or the most righteous, but they are your own. Problems develop when you think your views and ways of living life are superior or exclusively correct and you try to force them onto others.

Do not place yourself on a pedestal by thinking *your* point of view is irrefutably correct or *your* beliefs are absolutely right. I call this type of thinking the "Me People Complex." It stems from the selfish perspective in which people are unable or unwilling to view things from someone else's point of view. This complex is exemplified very well by what I like to call the "I'm the only one who knows how to drive!" syndrome. Driving is a most useful example for demonstrating the self-centeredness of people because it so readily brings out our undesirable tendencies. There is nothing like getting behind the wheel of a car to bring out our impatience, selfishness, anger, self-righteousness, and intolerance. This syndrome is illustrated by driving but the principles it demonstrates apply to every aspect of life.

"I'm the only one who knows how to drive!"

The description of this syndrome is as follows:
Does this sound like you?

When you drive down the road you tend to see *your* immediate needs and no one else's. You may believe that the other travelers around you do not need to get to where they are going as badly as you do. Their right to be on the road is definitely not as important as yours. *You* have to do what *you* have to do in order for *you* to get to where *you* are going. Do you see a pattern here? If you suffer from this syndrome, you honestly believe your perspective and view is exclusively correct.

Syndrome Example 1: Imagine you are in a hurry but the car in front of you is going almost exactly at the speed limit.

Does that driver's "slow driving" begin to irritate you? Do you start to tailgate the car, thinking, "C'mon! Can't you see that I'm in a hurry? SPEED UP!" At a stoplight or stop sign you may think that the driver is taking an extraordinarily long time to get going — maybe just to tick you off a little bit. Now, anger and intolerance have entered the picture. That person could drive faster! After all, *your* need to reach *your* destination is more important than another driver's right to observe the speed limit because *your* needs come first. Think about why you are angry. What is the other person really doing wrong? How would you feel if you were treated with this same type of intolerance?

Turn the example around: You've had a rough day. In order to relax and unwind, you plan to take a nice, leisurely ride home. You are traveling at the speed limit or perhaps a little faster when you notice a pair of headlights in the rearview mirror. The light becomes increasingly brighter as the car gets closer...and closer still. Finally it is so close that a tap of your brake pedal would certainly cause a collision. What is this driver doing? What a jerk! Some people are so impatient! Your right to drive the speed limit is more important than the tailgater's desire to get to his or her destination faster. Once again, your needs are more important, and your perspective is exclusively correct.

Do you remember the first part of the example? Is it okay if you are intolerant or impatient with someone else when it suits your needs, but not okay when those things are done to you? If you recognize yourself in these scenarios, take the opportunity to identify and address your actions and attitudes of intolerance. Try on the other guy's driving gloves and view things for a minute from his perspective.

****

If you are feeling that your needs are always most important, you cannot be tolerant of others. If you believe that people who don't conform to your needs are misguided, you place yourself squarely into a narrow, intolerant, selfish point of view.

****

Syndrome Example 2: This scenario starts when you are driving down the open road. Suddenly, someone turns onto the road right in front of you. You have to slam on the brakes to avoid a collision. To top things off, the inconsiderate driver in front of you seems to be taking forever to get up to speed. You tailgate the bumper to make sure he knows you are upset, and you think, "That unbelievable "#@*&!@#$*^&% so-and-so!" Your blood pressure is up, you are upset, and the way you are driving unquestionably shows your anger. "What an inconsiderate driver! He is definitely wrong," you say (possibly with a little stronger language). While that may be true, you should remember to give that driver some space.

"Why should I?" you may ask. "A driver should know better! This is my lane! That's unacceptable! A driver like that shouldn't be allowed on the road." First of all, RELAX! There is no reason to become upset, territorial, or impatient over petty things as quickly as many people do. Everybody makes mistakes. Have patience. Be tolerant and understanding about the mistakes of others because you want and deserve that same tolerance for yourself — don't you? Learn to give others the benefit of the doubt and treat the shortcomings and mistakes of others with the same amount of tolerance you afford yourself.

Turn this second example around: If you were to pull out in front of someone thinking you had plenty of time to do so (but really didn't) you would undoubtedly appreciate another driver giving you some slack (tolerance). How would you feel if the driver you just cut off were to flash the bright lights and crawl up your bumper? Do *they* then become "the jerk?" Do you think, "Can't they understand? I thought I had more time. I just made an error in judgment! What an impatient "&^%#*!" In other words, do you give the same amount of patience and understanding to others that you afford yourself?

****

Apply these principles to every aspect of life and recognize your actions of intolerance. Give the same amount of patience, tolerance, and understanding to others that you want for yourself.

****

Now that you have had the opportunity to think about these scenarios, consider the following questions. Do you often blame *"They - Them - Him - Her – She – He - It - Them - They?"* Is it always someone or something else that is at fault? Do you notice that everyone else has faults and makes bad mistakes? You may think, "I don't make many mistakes or have many faults. Well, at least mine are not as bad as other peoples'." While your mistakes and faults may not seem so bad, that's because they do not seem so bad to *you*. When you only have tolerance for yourself, you immediately become intolerant of others.

Do you dislike certain ways people treat you, only to turn around and act the same way toward others? Are you able to find justification for your mistakes easily? Do you readily offer tolerance for the mistakes and shortcomings of others? Ask yourself these questions and answer them honestly.

Ironically, the worst perpetrators of personal intolerance are often the most inept in dealing with the intolerance aimed toward them.

****

Many of us feel that other people are often at fault, wrong, or misguided. This is demonstrated when we are too critical of the shortcomings and mistakes of others, while forgetting or minimizing our own weaknesses, faults, and errors. Learn to place yourself in the shoes of others in order to become more tolerant.

****

Don't be too quick to point out the shortcomings of others. Instead, take the high-powered binoculars of criticism that so deftly point out the faults of others and view yourself through them. You will see that you have just as many (if not more) faults. Accept the fact that you are no better than the person next to you. When you recognize this, you will find it harder to feel intolerant of others. Above all, learn to view situations through the eyes and perspectives of other people.

~ Spiritual Tolerance ~

Spirituality is very personal and deep-rooted, so discussion of our views often leads to intense debates, disagreements, or arguments. Spiritual convictions and views are often so strong and profound that we can find it virtually impossible to tolerate and respect different outlooks. Nevertheless, living with goodness dictates that we become as tolerant as possible in every aspect of our existence, especially those concerning spiritual beliefs.

Throughout the world, various cultures and individuals maintain unique perspectives of SomeThing Greater. There

111

are countless personal beliefs and belief systems but people sometimes have trouble accepting the fact that there can be more than one spiritual path available. All true beliefs are fundamentally similar, sharing many universal ideas, ideals, and guidelines. (See Chapter 9 for a detailed look at this topic.)

Human beings naturally view things differently from one another, but spiritual views can easily become selfishly skewed. Many people spend time and energy trying to prove why *their way* of thinking or believing is the solitary, exclusive path to God. These attitudes can be shown outwardly or expressed subtly. Thinking in such a way sours spiritual belief with intolerance and separation, causing the intent and purpose of true faith to become lost.

Intolerance leads away from goodness. Problems begin to surface when people try to force their convictions upon others. Remember, just as there are many different languages, many different ways to set up governments, many ways to exhibit culture, and to express feelings and facts, there are many interpretations of religious and spiritual beliefs. If you express faith in your own way, it is important to allow others to express faith in their own way, as well.

To learn tolerance, spend time exploring other views of faith. Extend goodness and helpfulness toward others through your spiritual beliefs. The task of fostering goodness is more important than arguing about which belief is the only "right" one. Focus your energy on what truly matters — connecting spiritually in order to foster goodness.

Countless belief systems, traditions, and perspectives are valid as long as they do not promote hateful, intolerant, or harmful behaviors. You may not have knowledge of differing beliefs or feel completely comfortable with other spiritual customs or views, but spiritual tolerance does not ask you to believe or worship in a different way. Spiritual tolerance asks that you be open to the fact that other people may connect with God in their own way. You are doing no disservice to your faith by being tolerant of other true beliefs. On the contrary, being tolerant is an act of goodness that true faith expects and requires from you.

~ Become Tolerant ~

Stem the tide of intolerance in your mind. First, recognize why intolerance exists in your life. If you are intolerant of the outward appearance of another person, you must remind yourself that others must tolerate the way you look. If you do not like the personality or beliefs of another person, remember that your personality and beliefs have to be tolerated by others as well. You simply do not have the right to be intolerant of others because of differences.

Can someone force you to stop being intolerant? The answer is a resounding *no*. If you choose to be intolerant about certain things, no amount of reading or talking about how you should take the moral high ground will change your perspective. That change must come from within you. You have a choice to tolerate the differences of others — it is *your* choice. Do not wait until it is too late for you to change your behavior.

In order to get back to good, be tolerant. It is the right thing to do. It is good. However, if you take a tolerant view, there is no guarantee that others will do the same for you. In the real world, you will face intolerance in some form. Be the bigger person and show tolerance to the best of your ability. Eventually, the same end awaits everyone; therefore, it is important to be tolerant along the way.

~ Give Help ~

There is a constant ebb and flow throughout the world regarding what people have, what people need, and what people have to give. People can be strong at times, yet weak or helpless at other times under different circumstances. Out of that imbalance comes our responsibility and our opportunity to help one another.

The ways in which we can help one another are as vast and varied as the number of people on earth. Each person can offer help in a unique way. Helping ranges from giving time or money to being genuinely kind; from helping a troubled youth to showing compassion; from lending a sympathetic ear to adopting a child, as well as everything in between. Some people feel comfortable volunteering in a program that benefits a specific cause, while others give by donating their time or expertise through larger organizations. Still others can help by writing a check, which is volunteering in a different way. No form of help is too big or small. Each of us can give help by offering kindness, respect, and tolerance.

Offering to lend a hand to someone is one of the best things you can do. When some aspects of your life are going well, as when you may be enjoying good health, stable finances, or good cheer, share some of that good fortune by directing it toward other people. If life is not going so well, try to give even if you feel you cannot. When you do not have time to give, find another way, such as giving money or kindness. All means of giving are important.

While each person shares the responsibility to be helpful, we are not all destined to give in the same ways. Do not measure your gifts of help against the gifts of others; give to the best of *your* ability. Help may go to family members and people you come across daily, as well as to others you may not know in more distant places.

Learn to offer help because you want to, because it fosters goodness, not because you expect to gain from it or so that others may see the good you have done. Do not brag about any help you have given, or make a recipient of your helpfulness feel as if they owe you. Remember, when you help someone, you are fulfilling a part of your responsibility for goodness. It is the right thing to do. It is good.

~ Give Forgiveness ~

To forgive is to let go, to choose to replace your feelings of anger and hurt with the calmness and peace of mind that forgiveness affords you. Forgiveness can change negative feelings, emotions, and actions into positive ones and is something that you "own" to give to others. Undoubtedly, there are times when forgiving is difficult, but the benefits of forgiveness far outweigh any difficulties involved. Forgiveness can repair relationships, remove stress and negativity, and move you closer to goodness.

Over the course of our lives, every one of us will become hurt and angered by the words, thoughts, and actions of fellow human beings or by forces of nature. When you are hurt, angry, or in anguish, you move through a natural process to deal with those feelings. You may feel fury or detachment from whomever or whatever has caused your pain. Those feelings may turn into grudges and breed negativity in your attitude, well-being, and treatment of others. Such feelings are unhealthy and take away from your ability to foster goodness. One way to combat this negativity is to grant true forgiveness.

Forgiving can be difficult to do. The pain or hurt can run so deep or be so emotionally scarring that forgiving can seem virtually impossible. Releasing a grudge and offering forgiveness may not be the first thing that comes to your mind when you are hurt and angered, but eventually it is possible. There are no timetables or specific steps that can be taken to hasten forgiveness because there are subtle and major differences that affect every situation and every person in unique ways.

~ Types of Forgiveness ~

Two types of forgiveness exist, and are different in regard to relationships and situations. Both types of forgiveness produce similar results, and the benefits for you are absolutely positive.

—Type I Forgiveness — Forgive *and* Forget: The defining characteristics of Type I Forgiveness allow you to harness the positive power of forgiveness to continue in a healthy, productive relationship with someone who may have hurt, offended, or harmed you. Many different factors can either help or hinder Type I Forgiveness, the most important of which is your attitude and ability to forgive. If you are a forgiving person by nature and you can shrug off negativity quite easily, forgiving and forgetting will come naturally for you. However, if you have trouble letting go and offering forgiveness readily, you may have a tougher time. Extremely difficult circumstances and situations often cannot simply be forgiven and forgotten. In these cases you will need to explore a different type of forgiveness.

—Type II Forgiveness — Forgive *to* Forget: Sometimes the situation may be so difficult you cannot simply forgive and forget. Your hurt, pain, and anger may be so devastating that forgiving and forgetting is virtually impossible for you. Maybe the person who caused your pain is unwilling or unable to offer an apology or doesn't acknowledge any wrongdoing. Maybe you have lost contact, or the person may even have passed on. Type II Forgiveness can help you deal with situations involving other people, and it can also help you deal with circumstances and situations that are out of your control. When a force of nature causes devastation, or when you or a loved one suffers physical illness, there is no one for you to blame, no one who can offer you an apology. By learning to forgive and let go, you will be able to focus on your positive attitude and your responsibility for goodness.

When forgiving *and* forgetting is not possible, forgiving *to* forget can give you a way to work through the negativity that is sometimes inescapable. Although you may not be able to forgive directly for any number of reasons, you are in effect forgiving by letting go of the negativity associated with certain situations. Type II Forgiveness removes negativity in order for you to move on in a healthier, more positive way.

~ Try to Forgive ~

With your connection to goodness, your perspective of thankfulness, and your selfless attitude, reflect on the reasons why you should forgive, and try your best to do so. Remember to pay particular attention to your thankful checklist and be grateful for what you have received. Even if you cannot forgive readily or completely it is important to keep trying. Put this task on your conscience pest list. (See chapter 10.)

Challenge yourself to be a bigger person by forgiving as much and as often as you can. Of course, you will not be able to forgive readily in every circumstance, but try your best. Forgiving and releasing grudges forces negative emotions out of your mind so that positive thoughts, emotions, and feelings can more easily help you foster goodness.

There will certainly be moments when other people do not understand what hurts you. Sometimes they simply do not care. You will not get apologies or sincere explanations for many things that cause you pain. Sometimes other people cause problems, but some situations are just negative facts of life with which you must deal. When you have trouble forgiving, remember that you have done, or will do things that offend, anger, or hurt others. If you desire forgiveness for your mistakes, you must forgive and release grudges to the best of your ability.

When you are able to forgive, be sure to offer it in a true and complete manner. Do not hastily claim you have forgiven someone and then hold it over that person's head. Do not make those you have forgiven feel as if they owe you. Acting in such a manner means you have not truly forgiven.

~ Give Apologies ~

Apologies can build bridges across gaps or faults in relationships and they can heal wounds that have been created. An apology can go a long way toward repairing and restoring relationships and situations. A true apology, by its very nature, shows you are sorry for what you have done, and just as importantly, that you do not intend to do the same thing again. When giving a sincere apology, you understand that you have brought some kind of pain or offense to someone and sincerely empathize with the hurt they feel. A true apology means that you will try in earnest to stop the behavior or actions that necessitated the apology in the first place.

When you offend or cause pain, you must be the one to make the effort to offer a heartfelt, sincere apology. If you have wronged someone, apologize. If a person believes that you have wronged him or her, try to get to the source of the problem and offer an apology for any misunderstanding. This may not always be practical or plausible, but it can work wonders to repair relationships and bring a positive energy and attitude to all involved.

****

Simply because something would not offend or hurt you does not mean it cannot offend someone else. Be aware of what you say and do to others. If they are hurt by your words or actions, set aside your pride, apologize, and ask for forgiveness.

****

When you act in ways that are hurtful to others, the only way to correct the situation is to go to the person and admit that what you have done was wrong. Then, offer a sincere apology. Remember, a sincere apology is not simply lip service, it shows that you understand and empathize with the hurt you have caused. Once you apologize, you are required to make every effort to stop the offending behavior.

This step is a very important factor in repairing relationships and encouraging forgiveness. When you offer a sincere apology, you make it much easier for another person to forgive and forget. Complete forgiveness will become a much longer and more difficult process if the "offender" does not make a sincere apology.

~ Give Kindness ~

Giving is complete when it is carried out with kindness. Kindness is a trait that lives within the human spirit. Although it may not always be readily evident, the ability to be kind is an extension of the goodness that is part of human nature. Kindness can be something that is given outwardly, such as helping others in a caring, compassionate way, or by giving sympathy, forgiveness, and love. In other instances, kindness is less obvious but no less important. Less obvious ways of offering kindness include holding your anger in check — even if you have the right to be angry; tempering your words to

119

prevent an argument from starting; or backing down once one has started. Other ways to offer kindness include being polite to a person you do not really care for, expressing tolerance, and maintaining your composure and patience when dealing with the mistakes or shortcomings of others.

Billions of acts of kindness can occur when we simply change the way we face annoying, everyday situations. We often get irritated with people who can't control the very situations that cause us grief. Usually, they are just innocent bystanders. For instance, if you are at a crowded restaurant and your food takes a long time to arrive at the table, do you become angry and take it out on the server? Do you get upset at the telephone repair technician who shows up to fix your phone line because you are angry that the line is in trouble? Do you become annoyed and intolerant of others in a crowded store even though you are a contributing factor to that crowded situation? Ask yourself if you should be getting angry with the people involved in these circumstances. Learn to direct your anger at the negative situations, rather than at the people who just happen to be around when you become annoyed.

Giving kindness instead of anger will benefit you as much as the person who receives it. Kindness brings peace and allows people to act with reason and their intellect instead of reacting with selfishness and negativity. Think of examples in your life where you lose patience and get angry too quickly with people who do not deserve it. By truly listening, being tolerant, saying thank you, and being patient, you can show kindness. Be kind by giving trust, politeness, respect, and the benefit of the doubt. Kindness, to any degree, yields huge amounts of goodness and every kind action is grand because of the exponential potential for goodness that exists within it.

~ Give Environmentally ~

Humankind has lived symbiotically with nature for millennia. Until relatively recently that relationship has been successful. However, due to our many technical and industrial advances, the Earth is in throes of ever-increasing pain. The equilibrium of nature is out of balance because of humanity. Signs are evident now, today, but many dire problems will not be evident for hundreds of years.

It is important for us to give back to our world as well as to each other. We consume our natural resources at an ever-increasing rate and we continue to pollute and poison the very nature that sustains us. We necessarily live "in the now" to care for our needs, but we must be more proactive about living for the future — so our grandchildren's grandchildren will be sustained by a healthy planet.

~ What Can be Done? ~

You can do many things to help you live with goodness toward our planet. First, you can educate yourself on environmental issues and support those in the political and business arenas who combat the poisoning of our world. Take it upon yourself to learn about the hundreds of different things you can do to support and nurture the environment.

Every day you can take part in giving back to the environment by recycling, preventing pollution, handling waste products properly, conserving energy and water, seeking renewable energy sources, incorporating environmentally friendly attitudes in your purchases, and reducing and reusing. This list is by no means all-inclusive, but you can visit the Internet at www.backtogood.org for great resources on this topic. Do your part to give environmentally.

We can only ignore the poisoning of our food and water and continue to consume our natural resources at the current alarming rates for so long before our actions affect everyone. Hurting and ignoring the very environment that sustains us brings distress and suffering to all.

~ **Give** ~

When you are willing to share with others, you have come to realize that life and all that goes with it is a blessing. The point is not how much you are able to give. The point is *to give*. Give of yourself because you truly want to help others and foster goodness. Give to others by nurturing our environment, offering help, and being tolerant and trusting. Offer patience and forgiveness. Truly listen to others and encourage with kindness. All ways to give are connected to one another, and they are all connected to our goal of getting back to good.

****

Remember to extend kindness when you give. If you give without kindness your giving is significantly reduced in value. If you give something and then take it back, begrudge your gift, or make people feel like they owe you for what you have given, it is better not to give at all.

****

Giving through beliefs and actions has an ever-expanding potential for bringing more goodness into our world. Once you have gained the ability to give of yourself without expectation of getting something in return, you have mastered an important purpose of life — selflessness. Do not miss an opportunity to make someone's day, week, year, or life a bit more enjoyable by showing that you care. Through your selfless gifts you can change someone's life!

Take care of yourself and your loved ones, take time out for yourself when you need to, and when you are able to, give, give, and then give some more. Give in any way, to any capacity. Life can be hard enough — do not make it more difficult by hindering goodness through negative thoughts and behaviors. Fulfill a major purpose of life by finding ways to give to others.

I am only one, but still I am one;
I cannot do everything, but still I can do something;
And just because I cannot do everything,
I will not refuse to do the something that I can do.
—Helen Keller

✓ To Do List: Get Back to Good by Giving:

❏ **Give personal tolerance:**
—Remember that no human being — including you — has the power to dictate issues of spirituality, lifestyle, or culture.
—Tolerate unique viewpoints, as long as they do not cause hate or harm.
—Be as tolerant of the shortcomings of others as you are of your own.
—Remember that your views are your own and do not force them upon others.

❏ **Give spiritual tolerance:**
—Understand and accept the fact that there are many different ways of connecting to God as long as goodness exists.
—Do not force your spiritual views upon others.
—Practice tolerance by remembering that your spiritual preference is not the only correct way to worship.

❏ **Find ways to identify and stop your intolerance.**

❏ **Give help to others:**
—Recognize that offering help is one of the best things you can do with your life.
—Remember to offer help in many different and unique ways.
—Do not miss an opportunity to help someone — you will need help someday.

❑ **Give forgiveness to others:**

—Replace your feelings of hurt and anger by forgiving.

—Forgive as a means to release grudges because they take away from your ability to foster goodness.

—Give Type II forgiveness to help you learn to offer Type I Forgiveness.

❑ **Give Kindness to others:**

—Allow the natural trait of kindness to surface and act with kindness in your daily life.

—Remember that every kind action becomes grand because of the exponential potential for goodness that it contains.

—Give with kindness.

❑ **Give Environmentally:**

—Do not waste our precious natural resources.

—Find ways to help our environment.

❑ **Create your own To-Do list — Giving.**

Notes:

_____

_____

_____

_____

_____

_____

_____

_____

_____

_____

_____

_____

_____

_____

CHAPTER 9

Spiritual Tolerance
Become tolerant.

"To work for the common good is the greatest creed."
—Woodrow Wilson

As this book took shape over the years, it became clear to me that spiritual tolerance is a very important and sensitive topic that must be dealt with openly and completely. This recognition led me to expand the section on spiritual tolerance in the previous chapter. In order to truly understand our common ties to goodness we must accept that spiritual tolerance is ultimately as important as a connection to God. Many people have strong spiritual convictions yet they fall short of living with goodness because they fail to be tolerant of differing spiritual views.

Throughout history, up to and including the present day, humanity has leaped to fight in the name of religious and spiritual beliefs. The very beliefs and ideologies that purport to teach us to be loving, caring, and tolerant individuals have ironically been skewed and twisted to become the root cause of many atrocities. Spiritual belief can be used improperly to segment and separate people from one another. This intolerance has led to unthinkable actions of violence and evil.

Since religious and spiritual beliefs are a philosophical, responsive topic, the importance of accepting the notion of different spiritual views must not be minimized. Purveyors of faith can become very emotional and selfish when faced with a concept of spirituality other than their own; however, living with goodness dictates an openness and tolerance of many unique spiritual views. Become tolerant of all true spiritual beliefs because there is an equal place for every one of them.

****

While people have unique, personal views of "SomeThing Greater," God and SomeThing Greater will be the Names used throughout the book. If these are not terms with which you're comfortable, then please use names and concepts that you deem appropriate for your situation and beliefs. Also, the words religion, belief system, and spirituality are used interchangeably; please use the words that best describe your beliefs or perspectives.

****

As the human family is bound together in its similar characteristics, the vast and varied spiritual beliefs and views of the world are bound to one another by similarities as well. True spiritual beliefs may vary in appearance or characteristics, but they fundamentally shed light on the same truth. Different routes may be taken in order to connect with God and tolerance of that fact is essential in order to live with true goodness.

****

A major purpose of spirituality is to connect with SomeThing Greater and live with goodness by being thankful, kind, respectful, and tolerant of one another. Human beings naturally view things in different ways. We must learn to accept those differences and honor the magnificent religious and spiritual diversity of our world. Help to bring about more goodness by living with spiritual tolerance.

~ **A Solitary, Exclusive Connection?** ~

One of the greatest challenges we face with regard to spirituality is the debate over the world's many different religious and spiritual outlooks. People may have trouble accepting the notion that more than one path to God is possible and the different expressions of belief may trouble them. We can see this by looking back at many of the selfish acts humans have inflicted upon one another in the name of spirituality.

Instead of focusing on the goodness that should come from every type of true spiritual belief, people often selfishly spend time and energy trying to prove or justify why one particular belief is the *only* correct way to pursue faith. This view can be shown outwardly, expressed subtly, or occur only in thought but thinking and acting in such a way to any degree sours and distorts spirituality with intolerance. Inevitably, intolerance causes people to lose focus on true teachings of goodness.

The basic teachings of any belief system can be misinterpreted and sidestepped in order to try and prove a solitary, exclusive connection to God. Sometimes it seems that this way of thinking can become the main objective for spiritual beliefs. In that case, members of that spiritual practice actually begin to suppress the teachings and principles of goodness. People who maintain this mindset fail to see the immense importance of goodness and tolerance as inherent components of spirituality. They become blinded by intolerance and selfishness and lose the ability to recognize the fundamental objectives of true faith, as well as the universal similarities of goodness that all true beliefs share.

Spirituality is a very personal, passionate, and profound aspect of life. People can delve into the details and particulars of certain beliefs, and that's okay as long as the major focus is on a spiritual connection *and* living with goodness. Without such a focus, people may become intolerant and self-serving, or even grow to be uncompromising through selfish ideologies. If you claim a selfishly exclusive connection to God you can easily begin to target other beliefs or spiritual perspectives with intolerance.

~ Intolerance is Ignorance ~
Ignorance is Intolerance

People come to know and connect with God in many different ways. Some people are raised with a certain belief while others may find a path to spirituality later in life. When a spiritual belief teaches of SomeThing Greater, promotes goodness and tolerance, and feels right for an individual, a true spiritual connection has been achieved. However, when a person believes his or her specific belief is the only correct way to worship, intolerance diminishes the association to goodness and the spiritual connection is lessened along with it.

****

A "tunnel vision" perspective of spirituality can lead you to focus too narrowly. Other views or beliefs may not be discovered or acknowledged and they can even become objects of intolerance.

****

I suffered from spiritual ignorance in my own life. The only thing I knew about spirituality was what I had been raised to believe. I had heard of differing belief systems in my youth but I thoroughly believed my own religion was the one path that God wanted humanity to follow. To be quite honest, I never gave the topic too much thought and I never bothered to open my mind to the fact that other beliefs could connect with God.

131

I finally began to notice differing spiritual views when I was looking through a pamphlet comparing many different religions and belief systems. The pamphlet gave general summaries of each belief, together with the corresponding doctrine or basic convictions. The wake-up call for me came when I realized the most obvious fact — different beliefs taught and expressed fundamentally similar ideas and ideals of goodness and God. Only the words, names, and specific rituals of worship were different.

Although I recognized the underlying similarities in all the belief systems listed in the pamphlet, I could see that many of them proclaimed their own infallibility as the way to connect with God. If you did not express faith in a particular belief explicitly you would face some sort of punishment for your lack of faith in the "right" spiritual belief. The fact that so many different belief systems shared this same assumption presented a problem to me.

I began to ask questions. Is it possible that one particular belief could be the only way to connect with God to the exclusion of all others? If that were true, then the vast majority of people in the world are not able to connect. If only one way was exclusively right, *then every other way was wrong.* What spiritual view has the ultimate authority to claim to be the only true path?

As these spiritual questions grew more intense, I looked to others more learned than myself to help me find answers. I sought people of differing beliefs and backgrounds and asked, "What belief is truly able to connect with God?" I found that many people were quick to answer, "My belief is the only one, because the holy texts of my belief say so, and they are the word of God." This statement did not satisfactorily answer my question because so many different beliefs claimed to have the word of God within their sacred texts. The answers did begin enlighten me to the fact that people can become very possessive of their spiritual views and ignorant or intolerant of spiritual views that differ from their own.

~ Different Holy Texts and "The Word of God" ~

While many spiritual beliefs maintain the belief that their holy texts contain the word of God, I have come to learn that people can be rather intolerant of holy writings that are not of their own particular beliefs. I confronted this issue about thirteen years ago. I had a well-intentioned friend who told me I should believe in the religion he practiced or I would face certain, eternal damnation. I disagreed with him, stating that his view was not fair or inclusive. After all, people face differing circumstances in life, are exposed to different beliefs, and have individual personalities with unique views.

As our conversation progressed, I told him that I was not raised with the same beliefs that he practiced and had my own, personal beliefs and ways in which I was comfortable worshipping. He paid no attention to my objections and remained adamant about his position and philosophy. He kept insisting his way was the *only* way. I was not offended. I simply wanted to offer him a different perspective that would allow him to become open to the fact that there can be different ways to find a spiritual connection.

I asked him, "If people were raised in a completely different religion than yours, one which maintained the characteristics of a true belief, and they followed their religion, connected with God, and lived a life full of goodness, what would happen when they die?"

He promptly answered, "They will go to hell because whoever does not believe (my way) cannot truly know God."

I told him, "It's not fair to judge or exclude people of other beliefs or perspectives simply because their specific views might be different from yours. People live under different circumstances and are exposed to unique experiences throughout life. They may feel completely comfortable and connected in their true faith."

He would not consider a position other than his view. In effect he was telling me to believe what he believed because it is right. What he lost sight of was the fact that his view was right for him but not necessarily right for every other soul on the planet.

I then asked, "What if someone from a completely different belief approached you, and said that you must believe his way or you will face eternal damnation?"

He said, "I'd be offended, and tell him that he is wrong because my holy writings say differently and the holy writings of my belief are the word of God."

I replied, "Other beliefs also have holy writings, and their writings are as much the word of God to them as yours are to you. Their writings teach of God, goodness, and caring for others, which is fundamentally similar to the writings of your beliefs."

He then replied, "That may be true, but I know what my holy writings say, and they are the truth. That is what I believe."

"You are entitled to your beliefs," I told him, "but true faith also instructs you to be tolerant and to live with goodness. How can you belittle, pity, condemn, or be intolerant of other beliefs that teach of God and goodness simply because they do so in a way that's different from yours? Would the authors of your holy text want you to spend your time bickering and arguing over different beliefs or would they want you to have faith and live with goodness?"

"I never thought of it like that," he replied.

I did not change my friend's fundamental beliefs that day, nor did I intend to. I simply offered him a perspective of spiritual tolerance. He came to learn that his religion never specifically stated it was the only way to connect with God but its followers had selfishly interpreted and incorporated that belief into its teachings.

Eventually, he came to realize and accept that people of differing beliefs were the same as he. He recognized that we are all part of the human family and we have room for many types and styles of religious and spiritual beliefs, as long as they maintain characteristics of true faith. By accepting the fact that our differing views are integral to humanity, he started to view spirituality differently by learning to have spiritual tolerance. My friend came to understand that a spiritual connection is an individual choice that does not have to be the cause of intolerance. He no longer saw the need to proclaim his faith as the only way to God. Instead, he refocused the energy he spent on maintaining that belief and applied it toward his responsibility for goodness.

Some time later, I heard my friend engaged in conversation. "Who can definitively say which way is the exclusively correct way to worship or what set of holy writings are exclusively correct? Many different holy texts teach about God and goodness. We should be tolerant of that fact and concentrate on living with more goodness."

****

Would the author(s) of your holy texts want you to spend your time bickering and arguing over different beliefs, or would they want you to believe in God and spread goodness? Focus on the teachings of goodness that reside within your beliefs.

****

Spiritual tolerance is not demonstrated by claiming that the holy texts of one particular belief exclusively hold the "real" word of God above all other true beliefs. As long as a spiritual belief is true in that it acknowledges and teaches about SomeThing Greater and asks its followers to live with goodness, the word of God is alive. I have come to the conclusion that many different beliefs and holy texts contain the word of God by addressing the differences of humanity in unique ways so that we can collectively understand our commonality and responsibility to live with goodness.

****

If you do not share this opinion you may agree to disagree on this point. However, it is more important to remember to concentrate on your responsibility for living with goodness, and continue to become a more tolerant person in every aspect of life, especially spiritually.

****

The writings of many belief systems are based on other religions. Like the Christian Bible, they may be based on earlier faiths and include extensions of those earlier holy texts. There are even differing versions and interpretations of the same texts within particular belief systems. The words, writings, and stories may differ in some ways, but the messages ultimately teach about God and living with goodness. Many holy writings teach the same fundamental ideals from different angles and perspectives. These differences allow the Word of God — words of goodness — to reach every person in every culture and society around the world.

~ Many Paths, One Destination ~

Logic tells us that there is more than one correct way to accomplish anything. Any procedure, process, or goal can be achieved from more than one direction. For example, there is more than one way to fly. In nature alone, different species in various genera have the ability to fly and each creature has a unique way to accomplish this task. Birds, insects, and mammals each have the natural ability to fly and use different methods to do so. Although human beings cannot fly naturally, we have learned how to fly in planes, helicopters, and hot air balloons. Each method of flying is simply a unique means to the same ultimate end of flight. The same logic applies to religious and spiritual belief. Just as there are many ways to accomplish the act of flight, there are many different paths through differing beliefs and views to reach the same ultimate destination of a spiritual connection.

The following example, "The Journey to God," illustrates the many avenues available to connect spiritually through differing beliefs. Every person's journey requires a unique style of belief because each of us has differing views, opinions, and personality. In addition, we face exclusive conditions, experiences, and circumstances throughout life. Every person must choose to find a personal path of spirituality that works for his or her individual circumstances and beliefs.

THE JOURNEY TO GOD: *Part I*

—Many paths to God:

Begin the Journey to God by imagining God at a particular physical location on Earth. That destination can be anywhere on the planet — on an island, on a grassy plain, in a small village or town, or on the 19th floor of an office building in a major city. Wherever it is, it is the same for everyone on Earth and each person who chooses to connect with God must travel physically to this location.

Since people live all over the planet they will have to come from many different locations and they will face various obstacles along the way. Some people will be physically close to God's location while others will be very far away. Some will have to navigate oceans while others may have nearly impassable land formations to traverse, and still others may only have to walk across the street.

Each person's journey will require something uniquely suited to his or her needs. Luckily, many different means and modes of transportation are available. Those who are able to reach God on land may only need a rolling vehicle of some kind. Others will need some sort of sailing vessel to cross bodies of water or may need to find a way to fly to the destination. Still others will have to use a combination of different travel methods to reach God's physical location.

In this Journey to God each of these differing travel methods represents a different system of true belief. Buddhism, Christianity, Hinduism, Islam, and Judaism are just a few of the countless true beliefs throughout the world. Each alternative method of travel represents a different spiritual belief because every method of travel is a different means to the same end. The functioning of a plane is different from the functioning of a car, and a car is different than a boat, yet all three methods serve the same underlying purpose of transportation. True beliefs can be as different as a car is to a plane and a plane is to a boat, yet they will achieve the same result — a connection with SomeThing Greater.

Alternative means of transportation differ from one another but they also share similarities in the fact that they follow common, fundamental rules. For instance, the law of gravity binds them. Gravity will keep an equal pull on everything

— planes, boats, cars, and people. Gravity treats every travel method equally and each method deals with its challenges in its own way. Each travel method also requires fuel. Fuel can range from wind power to jet fuel to food for the human body. Each fuel is different but it serves the same ultimate purpose.

Correspondingly, all true beliefs have rules and principles that are fundamentally similar. For example, the belief in SomeThing Greater binds all true beliefs the same way that gravity binds all travel methods. Different types of fuel can be compared to differing holy texts or doctrines that accomplish the same ultimate goals. Like modes of travel, all true beliefs have fundamental commonalities when you break them down into their basic principles.

THE JOURNEY TO GOD: *Part II*

—Each path has many forks in the road:

Although each path of true belief holds general, fundamentally similar principles, each one may have different specific characteristics or practices expressed through the diverse branches or groups that equate to forks in the road. Differing denominations or branches of a belief occur for many reasons and each is right as long as it retains the characteristics of a true belief.

Each travel method employed to reach God's physical location on Earth may involve many different choices. In the rolling vehicle category, you can drive a car or a truck, take a bus, ride a train, or even ride a bike. All of these modes are fundamentally similar because they all have wheels. However, they differ in the specific details of how those wheels are ultimately put into motion.

****

For illustrative purposes, I have chosen to represent Christianity as the rolling vehicle in the following example. This model works with any true belief system or true personal spiritual belief.

****

A fundamental belief for Christianity is the belief in Jesus Christ. This belief is what makes a person Christian, as opposed to another true belief. Christianity's wheels apply to cars, buses, trucks, trains, and bicycles, just as Christianity applies to Catholicism, Protestantism, Orthodoxy, and many other different branches. Christianity splits off into directions that are as different as cars are from trucks, trucks are from buses, and buses are from bikes. While those different views of Christianity are fundamentally similar due to the fact that they all have wheels, they differ in the specific ways those wheels are set in motion. Each type of Christian vehicle — the different branches — is similar to the others because each one has wheels representing its basic belief in Christ as savior.

Cars, trucks, buses, and bikes each represent a separate path for reaching God within Christianity. However, those paths can be further sectionalized. Take Protestantism, represented by cars. The different manufacturers of cars represent the diverse denominations of Protestantism. Each different manufacturer has a wide selection of models, which represent different worshiping styles within each denomination. Each model has different options representing personal views. In effect, by choosing a specific rolling vehicle, one can achieve a personal way to complete his or her Journey to God.

THE JOURNEY TO GOD: *Part III*

—Your connection is what works for you:

The way you choose to reach God's physical location on Earth is completely determined by your particular needs. You are the only person who can choose the mode of travel you need because only you know your unique, individual circumstances, experiences, and preferences.

If you determine that you need a rolling vehicle (your choice of belief) to reach God on Earth, you must choose the vehicle that suits your needs. If you choose a car (a particular branch) you will have to pick a manufacturer that suits your needs (particular denomination). Then, you will pick a model (a style or place of worship) that you like, with the options of your choice (your personal views and preferences) in order to reach your ultimate destination of God's location on the planet.

You are the only one who can determine if a car is necessary for your travel needs. That choice is perfectly suited to you and is the correct way *for you* to reach God. This does not mean your way is necessarily the correct way for another person. Different people face individual circumstances and experiences throughout life. In their Journey to God, they may have to travel differently than you do. For instance, if someone were on an island and had to cross water or a rugged mountain range to reach God, he or she obviously could not take a rolling vehicle like the one you chose. That person would require a different method of travel, but that method is no more right or wrong than yours. Each is simply unique means to the same end.

~ Different is Good ~

Most belief systems maintain that they are *the* way to God. Surprisingly, each true spiritual belief is correct to maintain such a conviction, because each one is in its own way, a path to God. *Every true belief is a unique way to reach the same end — a spiritual connection.* Because having differing beliefs is natural and normal for human beings, faith through spiritual belief is not meant to sectionalize humanity. Only selfishness and intolerance cause us to believe the path we have personally chosen is exclusively right.

Understandably, people can be passionate about spiritual beliefs. The passion they feel is natural and good as long as it is directed positively and results in thoughts and actions of goodness. If that passion separates us through intolerance of different true beliefs, spiritual views, or people, then it cannot be a true spiritual connection. Followers can focus on spiritual beliefs in a negative way that leads to unconstructive or even harmful thoughts and actions. These can range in varying degrees from simply believing your way is the only way to connect with God to becoming judgmental and filled with prejudice to the extreme of violence and murder in the name of a belief.

Intolerance and harmful behaviors are negative in their own right, but to commit these acts in the name of a spiritual belief is pure evil. These negative effects are not the intentions of true faith. Thankfully, relatively few people take their views to such extremes, although history reminds us of the devastation that can result when beliefs become extreme. We must always be mindful of the fact that even small actions and beliefs of intolerance are damaging.

~ Becoming Tolerant ~

One of the best things we can learn is to become as tolerant as possible in every aspect of our existence. This is especially important with respect to religious and spiritual tolerance because unique cultures, societies, and individuals maintain different perspectives of SomeThing Greater through countless systems and ideas of belief.

****

Spiritual tolerance asks you to be open to the fact that many different paths can connect with God. You are doing no disservice to your faith by being tolerant of true spiritual beliefs. On the contrary, being tolerant is an act of goodness that true faith expects and requires from you. If you do not know about different belief systems or spiritual views take it upon yourself to learn about them. True beliefs, no matter how different outwardly, are similar at a fundamental, universal level. Find these similarities and embrace the common factors while being tolerant of the differences.

****

If you believe your way is the *only* way to God, you are in effect saying everyone else in the world is wrong because every personal view is different. Even two people who practice the same religion in the same place have slightly different personal views of their beliefs. Whose view is exclusively correct? Yours? Mine? The person who believes one way or practices "this" spiritual belief? The person who believes another way or practices "that" religion? Keep an open mind toward other beliefs and views. Spend time learning about them and extending goodness and tolerance toward others. It is the apex of hypocrisy to claim to be a spiritually connected individual if you live without spiritual tolerance.

Faith can fill you with joy and happiness, and many people feel the need to express that fulfillment by telling others about it. This is completely normal and good — do not stop professing your faith. However, when you start to place your faith on a pedestal as the *only* correct way to connect with God, you are distorting the very reason for and essence of true faith. If you have a unique view about spirituality and you enjoy the freedom to express that view in a way that feels right for you, then offer that same choice to others. One important fact to remember is that *your* life is *your* personal journey to connect with God. That journey works well for you. It does not necessarily work the same way for anyone else.

Is it important for you to be allowed the choice to believe and worship as you see fit? If so, remember that it is just as important to allow others to express their spiritual connection in their own way. Would you like a person to tell you that a particular spiritual belief that is different from your own is the only true way to connect with God? If not, then be open to the fact that many paths can connect. Ultimately, it is more important to help others and to foster goodness than it is to argue about which religion or spiritual view is the exclusive, solitary connection.

Your responsibility is to give others the religious and spiritual freedom you want for yourself, not to become judge and jury by dictating a certain spiritual choice is the exclusive path to God. Do not dispute the particulars or specifics of differing beliefs, but instead focus on the fundamental similarities of goodness that all true beliefs and spiritual views share. Try to spend more time living with goodness, generosity, thankfulness, and humility.

****

If humanity put half of the energy and effort into practicing goodness that it spends in disagreeing about which belief is exclusively right, the world would be back to good.

****

Humanity has room for many differing spiritual beliefs and views as long as those views and beliefs foster goodness. Every true belief is simply a unique course that leads to the same end — a spiritual connection. One religion, belief, society, or culture cannot rightfully claim an exclusive, solitary connection because God is common to all. In the end, there is one truth — one destination — and many paths to reach that destination.

The Golden Rule
"Treat others as you want to be treated"
An important moral truth endorsed by
many of the world's great religions.

Baha'i Faith: Lay not on any soul a load that you would not wish to be laid upon you, and desire not for anyone the things you would not desire for yourself.
—Baha'u'llah, Gleanings

Buddhism: Treat not others in ways that you yourself would find hurtful.
—Udana-Varga 5, 18

Christianity: In everything, do to others as you would have them do to you; for this is the law and the prophets.
—Jesus, Matthew 7:12

Confucianism: …the basis of all good conduct…loving kindness. Do not do unto others what you do not want done to yourself.
—Analects 15.23

Hinduism: This is the sum of the Dharma (duty); do not do to others, what would cause pain if done to you.
—Mahabharata 5, 1517

Islam: Not one of you truly believes until you wish for others what you wish for yourself.
— The Prophet Muhammad, Hadith

Jainism: One should treat all creatures in the world as one would like to be treated.
—*Sutrakritanga, 1.11.33*

Judaism: What is hateful to you, do not do to your neighbor. This is the entire Law; all the rest is commentary.
—*Talmud, Shabbat 31a*

Native American Spirituality: All things are our relatives; what we do to everything, we do to ourselves. All is really one.
—*Black Elk*

Sikhism: I am a stranger to no one; and no one is a stranger to me. Indeed, I am a friend to all.
—*Guru Arjan Devji:AG. 1299*

Taoism: Regard your neighbor's gain as your own gain, and your neighbor's loss as your own loss.
—*T'ai Shang Kan Yin P'ien 213–218*

Unitarianism: We affirm and promote respect for the interdependent web of all existence of which we are a part.
—*Unitarian Principle*

Zoroastrian: Do not do unto others whatever is injurious to yourself.
—*Shayast-na-Shayast 13, 29*

✓ To Do List: Spiritual Tolerance

❑ **Become open to the fact that many true spiritual beliefs can connect with God:**

—Recognize that humanity, by nature, requires many differing spiritual views.

—Learn about and respect differing beliefs so you don't end up with spiritual tunnel vision.

❑ **Become tolerant of differing religious/spiritual views.**

—Remember that proclaiming one belief as the only way to God is not an act of spiritual tolerance.

—Recognize that intolerance of differing true beliefs obscures the basic meaning of faith.

❑ **Many paths, one destination — read "The Journey to God" again.**

❑ **Find *your* connection:**

—Find the travel method (belief) that works for you.

—Do not try to justify or force your travel method onto someone else because *your* travel choice suits *you.*

—Remember that your connection is yours alone. A rolling vehicle that may work for you will not work for other people if they require a boat or a plane.

❑ **Let others worship in their own way:**

—Extend to others the right you enjoy to worship in your own way.

❑ **Recognize differing, true beliefs:**

—In the end, there is one destination.

—There are many paths to reach that destination.

—All true paths are lined with goodness.

❑ **Create a personal To-Do List for your spiritual tolerance.**

Notes:

CHAPTER 10

Take Care

Care for your needs in order to help others to the best of your ability.

"Look to your health, and if you have it, praise God and value it next to a good conscience; for health is the second blessing we mortals are capable of..."
—Izaak Walton

In order to extend goodness to others, you have to take care of yourself. Before you can offer help and assistance you must feel healthy enough to do so. If you are not ready or able to give help you may end up being the one who needs it rather than the one who is giving it. As a person who is getting back to good, you must care for your own needs so you can promote goodness to the best of your ability.

Healthy attitudes, outlooks, and behaviors make you feel good. This, in turn, allows you to foster goodness to your full potential. On the other hand, ill health can nag at your body and mind to create negative feelings, perspectives, and physical conditions. Assess your life in every area and identify where you need to change for the better.

When you find an aspect of health that requires improvement, remember that help is available from many different sources. You can ask for support and guidance from friends, family, or health care professionals. Take stock of your health and realize that taking care is a vital component in fostering goodness. If you do not take care of yourself, all of the motivations to get back to good can mean little.

In order to give, you must feel healthy enough to do so. If you want to offer physical assistance to others, you must have the strength to do so. If you are lying ill in a hospital bed, you will not be able to offer much physical help to someone even though you can still help in other ways. Spiritual health is necessary before you can help others in a tolerant way with their spiritual health. You must achieve and maintain emotional health before you can persuasively encourage and uplift others. If you are depressed it will be difficult enough for you to maintain a positive or thankful outlook, let alone to pass those positive views onto others. Finally, consider the health of your conscience. If issues of conscience are bothering you and occupying your mind, you can lose focus on taking care and living with goodness.

While this chapter does not give you specific directions to obtain and maintain health, it does illustrate how important overall health is for you to promote goodness. Health is often taken for granted; while we have it, we may not give it a second thought. However, we quickly realize just how important a place good health occupies in our lives if we lose it. Learn to take care.

~ Physical Health ~

I cannot stress the significance of caring for your physical well-being enough. Losing just a small portion of your physical health will force you to notice its importance. A sprained back muscle can impair you for weeks at a time. The common cold, a headache, a toothache, or slight depression can make you suffer and long for good health. Small inconveniences like these can make you realize just how much you value and depend on feeling healthy, while a significant loss of health can really put life into perspective.

When your health is lost due to something beyond your control, such as an accident or illness, life can become difficult and painful. However, it is doubly disheartening and frustrating to lose health because of your own actions. While you may not be able to stop accidents from happening or change physical conditions that afflict you during your life, you are responsible to care for what *is* in your control — the way you treat your body. Learn to maintain good physical habits in order to have the best physical health possible. Living a healthy, wholesome lifestyle makes you feel good, thereby increasing your ability to foster goodness.

Good physical habits are an extremely important component of health, encompassing a wide variety of factors. Tasks such as eating properly, exercising, and caring for your physical condition all play a vital role in maintaining health. When you exercise, your brain releases endorphins that make you feel good naturally. Why? Because we are designed to be physically active — the body is healthier because of it. Natural, healthy foods are perfectly designed to fill you with just the right amounts of energy and nutrients, allowing your body to work to its full potential. Be conscious of your food choices, levels of exercise, and medical condition by incorporating healthy habits into your daily life.

While you work to improve your health by living a wholesome, well-rounded lifestyle, strive also to remove habits that have detrimental effects. Physical well-being is negatively affected by a lack of exercise, excessive drinking, excessive eating, smoking, lack of sleep, too much stress, and by using drugs of all kinds. You may choose to participate in such activities but negative habits ultimately work against you. If you overeat, drink excessively, and do not exercise, your body will let you know that it is being neglected. You may feel sick, sluggish, or nauseated, and your mental ability to focus and feel happy is diminished. These negative effects work to hinder the body's natural processes and ability to be healthy. Long-term abuses of your body can be very costly to your overall health and they will eventually catch up with you.

Assess the ways your physical habits affect your well-being. Poor physical health causes low self-esteem, irritability, and other negative feelings. When you need to adjust your physical condition, find a way to put that change into motion. You may be able to correct your problems alone, or perhaps you will need outside assistance. Either way can work, but in both cases the key to success is you. *You* must desire change. You may find it difficult to correct bad physical habits but you can meet this challenge.

Consider a wide range of issues when you decide to improve your physical health, from losing weight and exercising to quitting smoking or drinking; from reducing stress to becoming proactive with medical care. An entire assortment of books, seminars, medical facilities, and various programs can help you achieve and maintain physical health. Loved ones and friends can also offer you help and support in your efforts to gain good health. All of the information and infrastructure is in place, just waiting for you to put it into action. Caring for yourself physically allows positive benefits to flow into all aspects of your life.

~ Spiritual Health ~

When you are spiritually healthy, you will find peace of mind because you feel connected to SomeThing Greater. Spiritual well-being allows you to view life with tranquility and comfort because you accept the fact that the majority of life is out of your hands. This perspective gives you a sense of peacefulness that permits your innate knowledge of goodness to become prevalent in thought and action. With good spiritual health, you can maintain a thankful perspective and always find purpose for life.

Basic tenets of goodness are associated with true spiritual health and they are not negotiable. You must not harm, hurt, hate, or be intolerant of others based on race, culture, physical appearance, or differing beliefs. Since spirituality is a choice, you are *choosing* to accept the responsibility for goodness that comes with it. Incorporate selflessness into your life through your spiritual connection, and realize that caring exclusively for yourself and your needs will never bring true spiritual health. A true connection to God commands that your actions of goodness toward others become just as important as your beliefs. Look beyond a self-serving connection.

There will be occasions when you act contrary to the goodness your spirituality requires of you. When this happens, accept the fact that you are not perfect — you are a human being bound to make mistakes. However, when you do falter in some way, spiritual health can help you correct your outlook and actions. No matter how you may have stumbled in your efforts to live with goodness, you can find a way to restore your spiritual health by thinking and acting with goodness.

Spirituality is not necessarily tied to a religion or belief system. It is a personal connection to goodness. No one can tell you how you should feel concerning your spiritual connection except for the fact that goodness must exist within it and through it. Only you know what path feels right and that path must be found and navigated by you. Please allow others the same freedom with their choices. Once you find and maintain your spiritual health you will be able to foster goodness to a higher degree.

If you have no spiritual connection or are confused about spirituality, seek guidance from another source. Direction can come from people, books, or any number of belief systems.

Help is available everywhere you turn, but you have to make the choice to seek it out. The motivation to find spiritual health has to come from within.

~ Emotional Health ~

Emotions play a vital role in your life. They allow you to process your experiences and help you cope and come to terms with the events in your life, both good and bad. Failing to control or direct your emotions can create undesirable thoughts and behaviors that may eventually lead to poor emotional health.

Emotions can easily overcome and overrule rational, logical thoughts and actions. For instance, if you are angry or sad, those emotions can override more positive, selfless thoughts and you may do or say things you normally would not. Negative emotions misdirect your focus on life and take away from your ability to foster goodness. When your emotions are uncontrolled or run astray, you may to act in ways that you may come to regret. Learn how to deal with emotions effectively and try not to let them overwhelm and override your rationale and positive perspective.

Even though life can be challenging, you are ultimately in control of your emotional health; however, if you feel that you need help, find a way to address that challenge. While emotional health is your responsibility, you do not have to find it or fix it alone — help is available. Seek it out and use it for your benefit.

****

A fine line separates emotional health from mental health. If you know of someone who may need help, go to him or her with encouragement and understanding and find a way to offer assistance.

****

Emotional well-being brings positive feelings of thankfulness, happiness, care, and love. Positive emotions allow you to focus on your life in beneficial ways, helping you to promote goodness. Do your best to maintain a positive attitude in everything you do.

~ **Financial Health** ~

Poor financial health can have a devastating effect on your overall health. When your finances are out of order, nearly every aspect of health can be negatively affected. The stress brought on by debt or other money related issues ties into your emotional health by causing physical symptoms of stress ranging from anxiety to nervousness to trouble sleeping. You may feel an enormous amount of pressure on your shoulders from financial worry.

****

Often, financial troubles are of our own making so we make a difficult situation worse by adding a sense of guilt and despair to an already difficult situation.

****

However, there is always a way out of the stranglehold of financial trouble. In order to find your way back to good you must address your financial health. The first step is to make wise choices when spending and purchasing. If you have problems with debt, you should seek advice and information. Do not be ashamed if your financial house is not in order. There is always light at the end of the tunnel — but first you must enter the tunnel. The only way to do that is to take control of your financial position.

You may seek guidance from your family, friends, any number of books on the topic, or by legal means. Most importantly, you may seek help, comfort, and guidance from your spiritual faith. Remember, a bad financial position is not the end of the world but an opportunity to fix up, renovate, and start anew. Once you begin, you will dramatically lighten the burden you carry and ease the amount of stress that you feel. Then, you will feel like yourself again and be able to treat others with more care, respect, and understanding.

~ Health of Conscience ~

A conscience that is not clear leads to a mind that is not clear. When your conscience bothers you, it takes positive energy away from you and negatively affects health. The energy that could be used to do something positive for yourself and others is wasted with feelings of guilt, sadness, anger, or anxiousness. These feelings stem from problems and situations you may have created or helped to create. If you fail to clear your conscience, you are forced to carry a heavy burden that will ultimately affect your mind, your spirit, and your overall health.

Do you suffer from conscience pests? Conscience pests are those thoughts that creep from your conscience into your mind, where they nag at you. They detract from your well-being by ruining concentration and focus and they can literally eat at you from the inside out. Have you ever hurt or angered someone? You may know you should apologize but until you do, your conscience may nag at you. Do you worry when you promise to do something for some else, but consistently put it off? Does someone deserve your forgiveness, yet you are not able to offer it? Should you say thanks to someone who has helped you in some way? Do you want to call someone with whom you have lost touch, yet have not done so? Have you been selfish and resistant to change — even though your conscience is telling you differently? Have you committed

159

hurtful, selfish, or destructive actions? You can probably think of many more conscience pests to add to this list.

If you have to spend time and energy repeatedly wrestling with conscience pests, work to clear them out of your mind by taking action to resolve the issues once and for all. Once the negativity is out of the way, the path is clear for you to redirect that energy into more positive thoughts, attitudes, and actions. You may muffle your conscience pests for years, but you will not be able to ignore them forever. One day you will have to face them.

Distractions from your conscience make you lose focus on your responsibility to think and act with goodness. Clearing your conscience will allow you to focus on getting back to good. Conscience pests are self-imposed burdens. Let go of your pride, anger, or guilt, and work to clear those pests out of your mind. Identify what you need to fix and take it upon yourself to make it right.

Do not wait until it is too late. Clear your conscience now. In an instant you can lose your opportunity to make amends forever. The everyday pressures of life give us all more than enough to worry about. You should not have to deal with self-inflicted, preventable stress or ill feelings. Let your conscience be your guide and heed the messages it gives you. It is designed to let you know what is right.

~ Take Care ~

As I stated earlier, maintaining aspects of good health gives you the capability to foster the most goodness possible. This chapter does not give you specific directions to maintain health, but it does illustrate the importance of overall health in your efforts to promote goodness.

The ways you choose to care for your health are personal decisions; however, no matter what choices you make, the desire and motivation ultimately must come from you. Many effective means are available to assist and guide you if you actively seek good health and commit to maintain it. Remember to be thankful for the health you have, and put it to good use by fostering goodness throughout your life. Take care.

✓ To Do List: Take Care

❑ **Improve and maintain physical health:**
 —Make healthy choices and incorporate exercise into your daily routine.
 —Care for medical conditions.
 —Limit bad influences on the body.
 —Seek help to maintain your physical health when necessary.

❑ **Improve and maintain spiritual health:**
 —Seek out ways to strengthen spiritual health.
 —Do not harm, hurt, or be intolerant of others.

❑ **Improve and maintain emotional health:**
 —Control your emotions so they don't overrule your thoughts and actions.
 —Stay positive in your focus on life.
 —Help others maintain emotional health.

❑ **Improve your financial condition.**
 —Make wise financial choices.
 —Seek advice, information, and help from family, friends, or professionals.

❑ **Clear your conscience:**
 —Find and fix things that weigh upon the health of your conscience.
 —Take action to resolve any issues you are responsible for — before it is too late.

❑ **Improve and maintain all aspects of health to the best of your ability.**

❑ **Use your health to foster goodness.**

❑ **List your conscience pests:**

❑ **Clear those conscience pests.**

Notes:

CHAPTER 11

Find Complete Purpose

Discover your complete sense
of meaning and purpose.

"Life's most urgent question is:
What are you doing for others?"
—Dr. Martin Luther King, Jr.

Human beings instinctively search for meaning. The way to fulfill this need is universally similar for every person, and yet at the same time, every individual must do so in his or her own unique way. The way you fulfill your life's purpose may look quite different from the way another person does because everyone faces unique circumstances and situations.

Different aspects of life must be satisfied in order to fulfill your complete purpose. For instance, having faith is not enough if you do so only for your own needs. Being thankful to God without being selfless is not enough. Being selfless without a spiritual connection is not enough. Caring for your own needs or simply living without giving to others is not enough. Achieving balance between your needs and your selfless responsibilities will help you find purpose.

When you are able to manage your needs and concerns, engage in successful relationships, reach your goals, and enjoy life, you may be fulfilling certain areas of purpose. However, fulfilling those areas alone is not enough to enable you to find complete meaning. You must make an effort to foster goodness while connecting spiritually, maintaining a thankful perspective, giving selflessly to others, and attaining your goals. Do not wait until your dying day to realize these facts.

In order to survive and care for your life, your loved ones, and your future, you have to engage in a lifestyle that you can directly benefit from. That is a fact. Your goals will include achieving a satisfying lifestyle and finding fulfilling ways to care for you and yours. The desire to feel secure earning your living, anticipating a bright future, and caring for your needs is normal, natural, and necessary, but these things alone will not allow you to find complete meaning.

You have a greater purpose for life than simply succeeding with your endeavors and goals. There is no question that you feel good when you achieve goals and dreams, but if those goals and dreams are only associated with material possessions, accomplishments, and titles, you will ultimately (sometimes painfully) learn that those things mean very little in the end. To live life solely for your own needs cannot fulfill your complete purpose.

When people *only* accomplish materialistic and self-serving goals in life, they may be satisfied for a period of time but something will be missing. No matter how much you cram into your life, a void will remain. This emptiness can be filled by living with goodness and selflessness because we are meant to connect with and promote goodness.

****

Selfless instincts combine with our spiritual instincts to form the human desire to give and care for others outside of basic, physical self-preservation. Follow and encourage these instincts.

****

While our material needs and desires are important, we must realize that other areas also require fulfillment in order for us to feel complete and whole. Having spiritual faith is necessary to fulfill one such area. We have a fundamental spiritual need to make a connection through belief, faith, and goodness and by maintaining a sense of thankfulness. Giving to others through selfless thoughts and actions helps you find meaning in your life. We must find a spiritual connection, carry out thoughts and actions of goodness, *and* achieve our goals and dreams in order to feel we have lived completely.

~ **Why Be Good?** ~

Fostering goodness is truly important, and doing so completes a major portion of the puzzle of life's purpose. Life is a balancing act between caring for your needs and your responsibility to live with goodness. Learn to let your selfless instincts guide your actions toward giving goodness in any and all of its aspects. When you reach the end of your life, the legacy that remains is in how selflessly you have treated others. Your thoughts and actions of goodness are what ultimately matter. A profound quote from Albert Pine speaks to this issue: "What we do for ourselves alone dies with us; what we do for others and the world remains, and is immortal." Truer words have never been spoken.

Why am I here? What's this life for? Have you asked these questions? Maybe you think, "I want to succeed. I want a house and family. I want to make it to the top. I just want to live *my* life." However, do you ever think about what will flash before your eyes as you exhale your last breath of air?

When you draw your last breath, what will your thoughts be?

—You probably won't be thinking about:

➢ Material possessions;

➢ Accomplishments, titles, or positions you may have achieved;

➢ How much money is in the bank;

➢ Whether or not you had the nicest home;

➢ Your status or position in life.

—You might be thinking strongly about:

➢ Your connection to God (or lack thereof);

➢ How you have (or have not) helped others during the course of your life;

➢ How you have (or have not) been selfless and good to others;

➢ Whether or not you were tolerant and giving.

Selfless thoughts and actions, no matter how big or small, are what you will take with you. It is easy to be skeptical about my claim since there is no scientific proof to support it. I can offer no measurable data on the subject, nor can I prove it with numeric values or equations. However, it always becomes clear in the final moments. People who are granted a second chance after a brush with death often make giving and promoting goodness their top priorities. Most people do not get a second chance. Recognize the need to live with goodness before it's too late.

~ Realize ~

Do not deprive yourself of the things you need to build a safe, secure, and enjoyable environment for you and your loved ones, but do remember to think about your responsibility for goodness. As you start incorporating more thoughts and beliefs of goodness into your daily life, remember that actions of selflessness must follow lest the beliefs mean nothing. Being able to look back on life knowing you have given to others is a great feeling — a feeling greater than you can completely understand now.

Recognize your blessings and allow your selfless instincts to accomplish what they are designed to do. Care for nature. Offer some of your health, time, money, emotional and spiritual well-being by giving them to others in some way. Learn to truly share. Strive to be generous, kind, trusting, and selfless as much as you possibly can.

Get Back to Good: Have faith and connect in your own spiritual way while being tolerant of the ways in which others do so. Be thankful for all that is in your life, become selfless, take care, and learn to give of yourself to others. Finally, treat others with the "Golden Rule" concept that is shared by all true beliefs. Strive to attain your goals, and your meaning for life can be fully realized. Find *your* purpose.

✓ To Do List: Find Complete Purpose

❏ **Define complete purpose for life:**
　—Reflect on what complete purpose means.
　—Identify and fulfill your needs.
　—Incorporate goodness into your life in order to find meaning.

❏ **Understand that there is more than a material aspect to life:**
　—Remember that you won't be worrying about material possessions or accomplishments on your deathbed.

❏ **Live with goodness by being selfless:**
　—Recognize that your selfless thoughts and actions, no matter how big or small, are what you *will* take with you.

❏ **Help to fulfill your complete purpose by getting back to good:**
　—Have faith.
　—Connect with God in your own way.
　—Be tolerant of the ways in which other people connect.
　—Be thankful.
　—Be selfless.
　—Learn to give.
　—Take care.
　—Treat others as you want to be treated.
　—Be Good.

Notes:

CHAPTER 12
On Your Way...

"Be the change you want to see in the world."
—Gandhi

All of us are capable of bringing more goodness into the world by caring for others and for our environment, by living with tolerance and kindness, and by controlling our selfishness. Each of us has something good to give whether materially or by giving a great, positive attitude. No matter what your goodness is, find a way to give some of it to others. Do it now, while you can. Do not wait.

When you give to someone out of the desire to give rather than from the need to receive, you have learned to give genuinely. Make a choice to extend goodness to others by being selfless and giving as much as possible. You may not need as much as you think you need and you may not want as much as you think you want. This life is a maze that must be navigated, and the only way to reach the true end is to make the correct choices of goodness. Be mindful of your actions, because your actions toward others return twice to you (what goes around comes around).

Simplicity is pure; simplicity is often truth. As complex and awe-inspiring as nature is, ultimately, we exist for simple reasons: to connect with SomeThing Greater, to tend to our lives, to care for nature, and to be good to one another. Fostering goodness is a major purpose and responsibility of life. Unfortunately, this truth can be easily ignored because no one can force a person to act upon it. You can exist (sometimes quite well, in a material sense) by taking care of you and yours exclusively, because living selfishly is an option you do have. The desire to get back to good is a choice *you* must make — it has to come from you. If you feel that living with goodness does not apply to you, you may change your mind when you are drawing your last breath.

Your spiritual connection means little unless you treat others with goodness. Strive to be good by being kind, generous, caring, and helpful to others to the best of your ability. The fact that you are trying to live with goodness in your life will earn rewards for you and for the lives you touch. Remember to say thanks every day, especially to God.

Realize that you are equal to everyone. When you truly understand and sincerely acknowledge that we are all equal, you will treat others the way they deserve to be treated — with selflessness, dignity, tolerance, respect, compassion, and kindness — just as you deserve to be treated. You may be more successful, have more money, or be smarter than others, but in the overall picture of life those things make no difference because everyone has the ability to offer help and teach others in unique ways.

Live your life, take care of yourself and your loved ones, take time out for yourself when you need to, and, when you are able to — give, give, and then give some more. Give in any way, to any capacity. Give time, help, and money; give tolerance and patience; and top it off by giving kindness. Give by not gossiping or criticizing, and by truly listening to what others have to say. Share your blessings.

~ Do Your Part to Bring the World Back to Good ~

The way in which you start your journey back to good does not make a difference. The most important thing is *to start*. You do not have to achieve prominence or be written about in the history books to reach fantastic goals of goodness. The lesser-known everyday acts of being kind, helpful, or patient with others are extremely important and they give birth to even more acts of goodness.

Goodness affects everything in an exponential way. If you do one good thing, even something as simple as driving courteously, saying thank you, or offering material help to someone in need, you are helping to bring more goodness into our world. In turn, those good actions can lead to more acts of goodness, such as repairing relationships or giving kindness, love, patience, forgiveness, and tolerance. Every good action is important and the world will be that much the better for it.

Set an example by living with goodness, but always allow others the freedom to find their own path back to good. Remember, it will mean different things to different people. There are religious, cultural, social, and personal differences that are good in their own way, and each can serve in some capacity to help bring humanity back to good. Be tolerant of ways that differ from your own and always remember the fact that there are more than six billion ways to accomplish almost everything on Earth.

Negativity will continue even when you foster goodness. Do not let that fact hinder your efforts. Of course, there will be occasions when you are treated without goodness and you may experience selfishness, intolerance, or cruelty. This is an unfortunate certainty. However, you must not use it as an excuse to extend bad behaviors or thoughts toward others. Live with goodness because it is the right thing to do, and not because you expect it in return.

Do not let the actions of others deter or detour *your* actions of goodness. When people are mean or nasty to you for no obvious reason, remember that their actions are usually based on jealousy, greed, ignorance or some other type of selfishness. Find a way to deal with the negativity others may force on you and treat them with kindness. Learn to realize when you are able to deal with negative circumstances, situations, and people, and learn to know when you must remove yourself from that negativity before it causes *you* to think and act negatively.

You can make the world a better place by remaining true to goodness. Of course, there will be times when you fall short and get discouraged by what others do, say, or think, so don't be too tough on yourself if you lose your way. Instead, work to find your way back to good. As I said before, you may not be able to end world hunger or bring world peace, but through your thoughts and actions of goodness, you will do your part to bring our world back to good. Every good thought and action is grand because of the exponential potential for goodness that exists within it.

What difference have you made in the world by living with goodness? The answer may be short or it may branch out and touch many lives. Only *you* can choose your answer! No one can force you to exhibit true, selfless goodness, but living without it means choosing to live for nothing. Ultimately, you alone are responsible and accountable for your actions.

****

Remember what initially drew you to open this book in the first place?

****

Who are you? Who do you want to be? Why should goodness be part of your life? Have you considered these questions truthfully? Life can appear to be so hard, demanding, and unfair that taking care of your needs leaves little time, ambition, or energy for being a kind, selfless, and giving person. Maybe you're convinced that your beliefs, values,

177

and persuasions are the only correct ways to think and live. What if you could take a step back from your opinions, circumstances, and daily routines, and learn to be more tolerant, kind, and grateful? What if, above all, you could learn to live with true goodness?

Reflect on your views and values and aspire to live with goodness. Remember, if your life has not fostered goodness in one form or another, then you have lived for nothing. Do you want to take that thought to the grave?

EPILOGUE

New Beginnings...

Do all the good you can,
By all the means you can,
In all the ways you can,
In all the places you can,
To all the people you can,
As long as ever you can.
—John Wesley

As more and more of the six billion souls on Earth understand and incorporate the universal goodness that each of us is responsible for, the world can get back to good. Now is the time for humanity as a whole, regardless of cultural, spiritual, and individual differences, to pull together and put goodness at the forefront of our thoughts and actions. Goodness creates strong people with integrity, honesty, righteousness, and love. This, in turn, creates loving families and the desire to care for others. As principles and actions of goodness become learned, re-learned, strengthened, and passed on, getting back to good can become an attainable goal for humanity.

Recognize opportunities to foster goodness in your life and act on them. Teach *and* learn about goodness from those around you; from your spiritual beliefs, from your family and friends, from children, and from others you encounter. Commit to live with goodness in every aspect of life. Get back to good, and goodness will flow through you into humanity.

From our collective differences to our fundamental similarities, from our unique, differing personal views and beliefs to the elements we share on a universal level, we are one and the same. No matter what our spiritual beliefs or status in society may be, we are bound to goodness. To think and live with goodness is written into our very being — etched onto our souls. We are in this life together and we all lease our lives from the very nature that sustains us.

Now is the time for you to make a difference of goodness in your life, which in turn makes a difference of goodness for humanity and our world. Remember, in the end *there is right.*

"My country is the world, and my religion is to do good."
—Thomas Paine

GOD

BLESS

HUMANITY!

Inspirations

Here are poems, stories, quotes and songs that have inspired me over the years. Although I have made every effort to find the authors for these works, I have sometimes been unsuccessful and therefore cite them as unknown.

The greatest joy . . . . Giving
The ugliest personality trait. . . . . Selfishness
The most satisfying work . . . . Helping Others
The most destructive habit. . . . . Worry
The worst thing to be without. . . . . Hope
The greatest problem to overcome . . . . Fear
The greatest asset. . . . . Faith
The greatest loss. . . . . Loss of Self-Respect
The most prized possession. . . . . Integrity
The most worthless emotion . . . . Self-Pity
The most contagious spirit . . . . Enthusiasm
The world's most powerful computer . . . . The Brain
The most crippling disease of failure. . . . . Excuses
The two most power-filled words . . . . "I Can !"
The two most difficult words to say . . . . "I'm sorry"
The deadliest weapon . . . . The Tongue
The greatest 'Shot in the Arm' . . . . Encouragement
The most dangerous pariah . . . . A Gossip
The most helpful thing to do. . . . . Forgive
The most powerful force in life. . . . . Love
The most beautiful attire . . . . A Smile
The most effective sleeping pill. . . . . Peace of Mind
The strongest channel of communication . . . . Prayer

The meaning of life To believe, connect, love, share, and help one another.

–Unknown

~ Inspiring Quotes ~

"You cannot do a kindness too soon, for you never know how soon it will be too late."
—Ralph Waldo Emerson

"We must not, in trying to think about how we can make a big difference, ignore the small daily differences we can make, which, over time, add up to big differences that we often cannot foresee."
—Marian Wright Edelman

"To put the world right in order, we must first put the nation in order; to put the nation in order, we must first put the family in order; to put the family in order, we must first cultivate our personal life; we must first set our hearts right."
—Confucius

"Unless we think of others and do something for them, we miss one of the greatest sources of happiness."
—Ray Lyman Wilbur

"Hungry not only for bread — but hungry for love. Naked not only for clothing — but naked for human dignity and respect. Homeless not only for want of a room of bricks — but homeless because of rejection."
—Mother Teresa

"It is not what we take up, but what we give up, that makes us rich."
—Henry Ward Beecher

"If you have much, give of your wealth; if you have little, give of your heart."
—Arabian Proverb

"The various features and aspects of human life, such as longevity, good health, success, happiness, and so forth, which we consider desirable, are all dependent on kindness and a good heart."
—The Dalai Lama

"Not he who has much is rich, but he who gives much."
—Erich Fromm

"Be the change you want to see in the world."
—Gandhi

"Life's most urgent question is: What are you doing for others?"
—Dr. Martin Luther King, Jr.

"Look to your health; and if you have it, praise God; and value it next to a good conscience; for health is the second blessing we mortals are capable of..."
—Izaak Walton

"To work for the common good is the greatest creed."
—Woodrow Wilson

"You make a living by what you get, but you make a life by what you give."
—Winston Churchill

"Only a life lived for others is worth living."
—Albert Einstein

"Gratitude is not only the greatest of virtues, but the parent of all the others."
—Marcus Tullius Cicero

"Science can purify religion from error and superstition. Religion can purify science from idolatry and false absolutes."
—Pope John Paul II

"Science is not only compatible with spirituality, it is a profound source of spirituality."
—Carl Sagan

It is not what they profess, but what they practice that makes them good.
—Greek Proverb

"The welfare of each is bound up in the welfare of all."
—Helen Keller

"The world is my country, and my religion is to do good."
—Thomas Paine

"Degrees" of Goodness

Education is not limited
to being formal in nature.

...

*Any degree of education, in and of itself, should
not engender
a feeling of being superior or infallibly
knowledgeable;
as we can always learn more, especially from one
another.*

...

Claiming to be a spiritual person does not
inevitably equate to being a "good person,"
or fighting the "good fight."

...

*Spirituality, in and of itself,
does not equal goodness*

...

Educate yourself with
what truly matters in life.

...

**Study, practice, and live with true, tolerant
GOODNESS
to the best of your ability.**

—*Ken Ferrara*

Here in the maddening
Maze of things,
When tossed by storm and flood;
To one fixed ground my
Spirit clings,
I know that God is Good...

—John G. Whittier

"How lovely to think that no one need wait a moment, we can start now, start slowly changing the world. How lovely that everyone, great and small, can make their contribution...how we can always, always give something, if only kindness."

—Anne Frank

Native American Wisdom
- A Tale of Two Wolves -

One evening an old Cherokee told his grandson about a battle that goes on inside people.

He said, "My son, the battle is between two wolves inside us all.

The first wolf is evil. It is anger, envy, jealousy, sorrow, regret, greed, arrogance, self-pity, guilt, resentment, inferiority, lies, false pride, superiority, and ego.

The second wolf is good. It is joy, peace, love, hope, serenity, humility, kindness, benevolence, empathy, generosity, truth, compassion, and faith."

The grandson thought about it for a moment and then asked his grandfather, "Which wolf wins?"

The old Cherokee simply replied, "The one you feed."

—Author unknown.

I am only one, but still I am one;
I cannot do everything, but still I can do something;
And just because I cannot do everything,
I will not refuse to do the something that I can do.

—Helen Keller

Do all the good you can,
By all the means you can,
In all the ways you can,
In all the places you can,
To all the people you can,
As long as ever you can.

—John Wesley

<u>GOD IS</u>

God is great,
God is good,
God is the Creator of the world.
God is big,
God is small,
God made us after all.
The trees, the land, and the sea,
Even the air that we breathe.
We know one thing is true,
God created me and you.
God is great,
God is good,
God is all.
God is big, God is awe,
And most importantly of all,
Know in your heart that GOD IS.

—Ken William

The following tale is paraphrased to the best of my recollection, and cited as unknown:

One day, God finally decided to let people know what happens after death. A group of people visited that next place, and truth be told, there really is a Heaven and a hell.

Heaven, to the surprise of the visitors, is a vast banquet hall with a table full of the most delicious food and drink ever seen. The table is very wide, and long enough to fit every soul that sits to eat. Everyone in Heaven gets hungry often and needs to eat several times each day. Luckily, there is always plenty of food and drink. Unfortunately, everyone has arms that are as long as the table is wide, and their arms cannot bend so they are unable to feed themselves.

Hell has the same configuration — people seated at a wide banquet table with the same unbendable arms. Delicious food graces this table also. The daily hunger for the people in hell is ravenous and painful. Luckily, hell has an abundance of food and drink for everyone.

In Heaven, everyone is able to eat and is cared for because everybody looks out for the needs of others by extending their arms to feed the person across the table from them. With the abundance that exists, no one ever leaves hungry or has to do without.

Down in hell, people are only concerned with trying to feed themselves. Since their arms do not bend, no one eats. They suffer the extreme pain of starvation because they *choose* not to extend their arms to each other and help one another eat, so everyone suffers. The abundance of food only serves to enhance their suffering. Even though there is always more than enough food to go around, selfish people only look out for their own needs, and would rather starve then try to help someone else. That is the philosophy of a selfish existence.

Our lives are not very different from that example of Heaven and hell. There is an abundance of good things in life that every person can enjoy, and more than enough to go around if we learn to perceive positively, truly share, and give to one another.

The bottom line is that we all need help at some point in life, and we are able to help others at different times or in different ways, *so we should help one another.* Simplistic? Maybe. However, these truths could not be more powerful. Everyone has areas in life that need improvement in order to bring us to that end. Let's work on this together!

It is not the critic who counts, nor the man who points out how the strong man stumbled or where the doer of deeds could have done them better. The credit belongs to the man who is actually in the arena, whose face is marred by dust and sweat and blood; who strives valiantly, who errs and comes short again and again, who knows the great enthusiasm, the great devotions, and spends himself in a worthy cause; who at the best knows in the end the triumph of high achievement, and who at the worst, if he fails, at least fails while daring greatly so that his place shall never be with those cold and timid souls who know neither victory nor defeat.
—President Theodore Roosevelt
Speech at the Sorbonne, Paris, April 23, 1910

Make A Difference!

The ability for you to make a difference in your life, the life of another person, and the state of our world is always within reach. Find ways in which you can share: mentor a child, give time and money, show patience with friends and family, sign up as an organ donor, or reach out to offer assistance to those in need.

Following are a few of my favorite organizations that provide you with an opportunity to make positive changes:

➢ Global Call to Action Against Poverty — www.whiteband.org

➢ The One Campaign — www.one.org

➢ Tolerance — www.tolerance.org

➢ Children International: www.children.org

➢ Environmental issues — www.earth911.org

Please visit www.backtogood.org on the web in order to find more outstanding organizations designed to help and inspire you to find more goodness in every aspect of your life. Backtogood.org is dedicated to adding more resources that will help people Make A Difference.

Journal:

Journal your feelings, dreams, goals, and aspirations on the following pages; have fun with this and make this journal an integral part of your journey back to good.

_____

_____

_____

_____

_____

_____

_____

_____

_____

_____

_____

_____

Journal:

<u>Journal:</u>

Journal:

Journal:

_____

_____

_____

_____

_____

_____

_____

_____

_____

_____

_____

_____

_____

_____

_____

Ken Ferrara

Journal:

Journal:

_____

_____

_____

_____

_____

_____

_____

_____

_____

_____

_____

_____

_____

_____

Journal:

Journal:

Journal: _____

Journal:

_____

_____

_____

_____

_____

_____

_____

_____

_____

_____

_____

_____

_____

_____

Ken Ferrara

Notes:

Notes:

Ken Ferrara

Notes:

Notes:

Notes:

Notes:

Debts of Gratitude

Thanks to God,

Thanks for giving all through many names, forms, words, interpretations, and faces. I understand and accept that each day that we see another sunrise is a gift, not something that is earned or even deserved. I am forever thankful for our ability to know, the power to love, the beauty of nature, and for the miracle of life.

To my wife,

Thanks for your constant support and encouragement. Through the years you helped me keep pen to paper and motivated me even when I pushed away. If not for you, my thoughts would still be scribbled onto scraps of paper instead of helping us. Thanks for your insight, endless patience, and ability to understand me. I love you.

To my kids,

Thanks for your stern hand in making sure I would finish — and for keeping our secret. You sacrificed many things because Dad was always "working on the book." You waited so patiently through my mood swings and procrastination, and took many, many trips to Great America with Mom until this final copy was ready. Well, here it is. Now we can practice basketball, fly kites, and build snowmen. I love you.

To my parents,

Thanks for your help over the years, your faith in me through all of my trials and mistakes, and for the countless hours you sat by my side, encouraging me. Although I was often the "Jack" of the family, the lessons I learned helped me

215

to understand and know. In this little paragraph, I cannot begin to express my gratitude to you for the love, compassion, and generosity you have shown me, ETY, Mom. Love, Ken

To my grandparents,

To Busia, Dziadzio, and Grammy: Thank you so much for your love and generosity. I will always carry your love and patience in my heart and soul. I am forever thankful for what you have given me and for what you continue to teach. I could not have completed this book without your help (especially recently, Busia). Love, Kenosha, Kenoosh, Ani-mal.

For the rest of my family,

Auntie; Jim, Karen and family; Sal, Joyce and family, Licha and family; Keith, Alice and family: Kissy and family; Sunshine; Gary, Dawn and family, Tom, Michelle and family. To Mike (Big Stix), Martha and Family; Jimmy, Julie, and family; To Avelline (for your insightful advice and support), Kurt and Tara, and to the rest of my close friends and family who are equally important, thank you for giving me the insight, knowledge, and experience I needed in order to complete this book. To Mike, Anita and family, and Renee and Joe, through our share of disagreements and differing views, you have allowed me to see more clearly what living with goodness truly means. Through your insights, words, and actions, you have helped illustrate a clear path to true goodness. I pray that we continue what we started. Good luck & God bless.

BACK

to

GOOD

*Six Billion Ways to Bring
Goodness into our World,*

One Person at a Time.

The following pages summarize the To Do Lists from each
of the chapters. Apply them to your life in order to get
Back to Good!

✓ To Do List: The Tie That Binds — Believe

☐ **Have faith in SomeThing Greater.**

☐ **Accept that science explains the "how" of nature, not the "why" of nature:**
—Science can decipher and explain processes and procedures.
—Science cannot explain what gives natural laws authority, nor will it be able to fully account for the origins of existence.

☐ **Find a tolerant, genuine connection to goodness.**

☐ **Use your faith as a path to goodness.**

✓ To Do List: Connect With Goodness

☐ **Fulfill your instinctual need to connect to SomeThing Greater.**

☐ **Realize the purpose of spirituality:**
—Connect to God with goodness.
—Focus on being thankful.
—Think and act with selflessness.
—Believe in Something Greater than humankind (and yourself).

☐ **Connect with goodness:**
—Choose the responsibility to act with goodness.
—Do not cause harm, be intolerant, act selfishly, or foster hatred, *especially* in the name of a spiritual belief.
—Negotiate any perceived problems in life with the courage a spiritual connection provides.

☐ **Focus on the true message of your connection:**
—Focus on being thankful, practicing your faith in earnest, acting kindly, and living with tolerance.
—Do not focus on the material aspects and specific practices of a spiritual belief to the point where you are not promoting goodness.

☐ **Become open to accepting that differing true beliefs are able connect with God:**
—Recognize that humanity, by nature, requires many differing spiritual views.

—Accept that more than one particular belief or view can connect with God.

—Understand that different religions, belief systems, and personal views of spirituality come in many styles, shapes, and sizes, in order to fit the differing needs and circumstances of humanity.

❑ **Become tolerant of differing spiritual views.**

—Foster goodness instead of proclaiming a particular spiritual belief as the only way to God.

—Illuminate the basic meaning of faith by showing tolerance of all true beliefs.

—Learn about and respect different true beliefs to avoid spiritual tunnel vision.

✓ <u>To Do List: Look Up — Be Thankful</u>

❑ **Look up — be thankful.**

❑ **Thank God:**
  —The foundation of a thankful perspective starts by giving thanks to God.

❑ **Be thankful for each new day:**
  —Every day is a gift — for you personally, as well as for the world.

❑ **Be thankful for your health:**
  —Remember that your health is ultimately not in your hands.
  —Recognize that health covers many different aspects.
  —Be thankful for the health with which you're blessed.

❑ **Be thankful for your abilities:**
  —Realize that your abilities are a gift.
  —Be humble as you remember that your accomplishments are not completely yours.

❑ **Remove obstacles that hinder a thankful perspective.**

❑ **Stop taking things for granted:**
  —Consciously think about and be grateful for what is in your life every day.
  —Show gratitude in thought as well as action.

❏ **Do not feel entitled to the things you receive from God.**

—Recognize that you are not entitled to health, happiness, or a good life from God — they are gifts you receive.

—Be thankful for, and humbled by, the gifts you receive.

❏ **Be willing to accept that adversity may strike at any time in life.**

❏ **Be thankful through tough times.**

—Always find something to be thankful for, no matter what situation you are going through.

—Find thankful ways to deal with tough situations.

❏ **Do not pity yourself because of circumstances in life:**

—View life with thankfulness instead of pity.

—Do not compare your problems with the problems of others.

—Be thankful, because your situation could always be worse.

—View adversity as something that will make you stronger.

—Be happy for others when good fortune embraces them.

❏ **Try not to worry about what cannot be controlled:**

—Learn what is yours to control because much of life is beyond your control.

—Do not get so caught up with the details of life that you forget to act with thankfulness and goodness.

—Convert the energy spent on worrying into thankful thoughts and actions.

❑ **Strengthen your thankful perspective.**

❑ **Create your "Things To Be Thankful For:" checklist:**

—Reflect on and write down everything you should be thankful for, from a new day, to health, to the goodness of humanity.

—Review your checklist several times a day and add to it often.

❑ **Maintain an attitude of gratitude to the best of your ability:**

—Take heart in the fact that people have gone through terrible situations and have been able to maintain a thankful perspective. So can you!

—Share some of the gifts you receive with others.

—Remember that a life clouded with selfishness cannot maintain a thankful perspective.

❑ **A thankful perspective must be coupled with thankful actions of goodness.**

✓ To Do List: Look Within to Change

❑ **Understand why selfishness exists:**
—Selfishness is wired into the mind for physical survival.

❑ **Understand why selflessness exists:**
  ❑ —Selflessness is wired into the mind for higher levels of self-preservation that are as important as the physical aspects of survival, if not more so.

❑ **Work to control your selfishness.**

❑ **Empower yourself to live with goodness by encouraging your selfless instincts.**

❑ **Identify selfish thoughts and behaviors, large and small:**
—Do not rationalize that you are not selfish simply because you have not broken any laws or committed significant actions of selfishness.
—Recognize that selfishness covers everything from physically hurting someone, to intolerance, to stealing, to making fun of someone.

❑ **Selfishness can be changed:**
—You are responsible for fostering goodness by replacing selfishness with selflessness.

❑ **Make a personal to-do list to encourage selflessness:**

✓ To Do List: Selfish to Selfless

❑ **Assess your thoughts and actions of selfishness.**

❑ **Rate yourself on the selfish/selfless scale:**
—Get an objective opinion to help you identify what you need to work on.
—List your selfish behaviors, make a plan, and commit to change your selfish thoughts and actions.

❑ **Be selfless to the best of your ability.**

❑ **Do not judge others with respect to their possessions or lifestyle, as long as no hurt or harm is caused:**
—Recognize that everyone is accountable for his or her own lifestyle and actions.

❑ **Ways that I am selfish:**
➤ _____
➤ _____

❑ **What I need to do in order to be more selfless:**
➤ _____
➤ _____

✓ To Do List: Get Back to Good by Giving:

❑ **Give personal tolerance:**

—Remember that no human being — including you — has the power to dictate issues of spirituality, lifestyle, or culture.

—Tolerate unique viewpoints as long as they do not cause hate or harm.

—Be as tolerant of the shortcomings of others as you are of your own.

—Remember that your views are your own and do not force them upon others.

❑ **Give spiritual tolerance:**

—Understand and accept the fact that there are many different ways of connecting to God as long as goodness exists.

—Do not force your spiritual views upon others.

—Practice tolerance by remembering that your spiritual preference is not the only correct way to worship.

❑ **Find ways to identify and stop your intolerance.**

❑ **Give help to others:**

—Recognize that offering help is one of the best things you can do with your life.

—Remember to offer help in many different and unique ways.

—Do not miss an opportunity to help someone — you will need help someday.

❑ **Give forgiveness to others:**

—Replace your feelings of hurt and anger by forgiving.

—Forgive as a means to release grudges because they take away from your ability to foster goodness.

—Give Type II forgiveness to help you learn to offer Type I Forgiveness.

❑ **Give Kindness to others:**

—Allow the natural trait of kindness to surface and act with kindness in your daily life.

—Remember that every kind action becomes grand because of the exponential potential for goodness that it contains.

—Give with kindness.

❑ **Give Environmentally:**

—Do not waste our precious natural resources.

—Find ways to help our environment.

❑ **Create your own To-Do list—Giving.**

✓ To Do List: Spiritual Tolerance

❏ **Become open to the fact that many true spiritual beliefs can connect with God:**
   —Recognize that humanity, by nature, requires many differing spiritual views.
   —Learn about and respect differing beliefs so you don't end up with spiritual tunnel vision.

❏ **Become tolerant of differing religious/spiritual views.**
   —Remember that proclaiming one belief as the only way to God is not an act of spiritual tolerance.
   —Recognize that intolerance of differing true beliefs obscures the basic meaning of faith.

❏ **Many paths, one destination — read "The Journey to God" again.**

❏ **Find your connection:**
   —Find the travel method (belief) that works for you.
   —Do not try to justify or force your travel method onto someone else because *your* travel choice suits *you.*
   —Remember that your connection is yours alone. A rolling vehicle that may work for you will not work for other people if they require a boat or a plane.

❏ **Let others worship in their own way:**
   —Extend to others the right you enjoy to worship in your own way.

❑ **Recognize differing, true beliefs:**
   —In the end, there is one destination.
   —There are many paths to reach that destination.
   —All true paths are lined with goodness.

❑ **Create a personal To-Do List for your spiritual tolerance.**

✓ To Do List: Take Care

❑ **Improve and maintain physical health:**
—Make healthy choices and incorporate exercise into your daily routine.
—Care for medical conditions.
—Limit bad influences on the body.
—Seek help to maintain your physical health when necessary.

❑ **Improve and maintain spiritual health:**
—Seek out ways to strengthen spiritual health.
—Do not harm, hurt, or be intolerant of others.

❑ **Improve and maintain emotional health:**
—Control your emotions so they don't overrule your thoughts and actions.
—Stay positive in your focus on life.
—Help others maintain emotional health.

❑ **Improve your financial condition.**
—Make wise financial choices.
—Seek advice, information, and help from family, friends, or professionals.

❑ **Clear your conscience:**
—Find and fix things that weigh upon the health of your conscience.
—Take action to resolve any issues you are responsible for — before it is too late.

❑ Improve and maintain all aspects of health to the best of your ability.

❑ Use your health to foster goodness.

❑ List your conscience pests:

❑ Clear those conscience pests.

✓ <u>To Do List: Find Complete Purpose</u>

❑ **Define complete purpose for life:**
—Reflect on what complete purpose means.
—Identify and fulfill your needs.
—Incorporate goodness into your life in order to find meaning.

❑ **Understand that there is more than a material aspect to life:**
—Remember that you won't be worrying about material possessions or accomplishments on your deathbed.

❑ **Live with goodness by being selfless:**
—Recognize that your selfless thoughts and actions, no matter how big or small, are what you *will* take with you.

❑ **Help to fulfill your complete purpose by getting back to good:**
—Have faith.
—Connect with God in your own way.
—Be tolerant of the ways in which other people connect.
—Be thankful.
—Be selfless.
—Learn to give.
—Take care.
—Treat others as you want to be treated.
—Be Good.

CONTACT INFO:

Did <u>Back to Good</u> help you?

I would love to hear from you regarding how you will get back to good. Here are some ideas and questions to get you started. Feel free to add your own!

- Has this book changed your perspective? If so, how?

- How have you incorporated the principles and ideas in the book with your beliefs and lifestyle?

- How do you plan to live with more goodness?

- Has *Back to Good* motivated you to volunteer additional time, tolerance, money, or kindness? If so, let me know how much so I can track the collective difference of goodness we are making in the world (check www. backtogood.com for results).

- How are you taking care? Have you been able to apologize to others and clear some of your conscience pests? Have you forgiven someone and improved your quality of life? Did you improve emotional, spiritual, or physical health in order to repair relationships and foster goodness?

- Do you offer more respect and care for nature and our environment?

233

Please reply at:

www.backtogood.com/goodnesssstracker.html

ORDER INFO:

Go to *www.backtogood.com* for more information, to send correspondence, and to purchase products and books that can help you get **Back to Good.**

Back to Good can be purchased at bookstores and booksellers everywhere!

Or call (888) 280-7715

Printed in the United States
73190LV00004B/80

9 781418 453466